The
KINGDOM
of God Is a
PARTY

Tony Campolo

Phil 3:14

Also by Tony Campolo
  Partly Right
  A Reasonable Faith
  It's Friday, but Sunday's Comin'
  You Can Make a Difference
  Who Switched the Price Tags?
  20 Hot Potatoes Christians Are Afraid to Touch

With Bart Campolo
  Things We Wish We Had Said

Tony Campolo

The

KINGDOM

of God Is a

PARTY

WORD PUBLISHING

Dallas·London·Vancouver·Melbourne

THE KINGDOM OF GOD IS A PARTY

Scripture quotations are from the King James Version of the Bible.

Library of Congress Cataloging-in-Publication Data

Campolo, Anthony.
     The kingdom of God is a party : God's radical plan for
   his family / Tony Campolo
     p. cm.
   ISBN 0–8499–0767–5
      0–8499–3399–4 (pbk.)
     1. Kingdom of God.   2. Christian Life—Baptist authors.
 I. Title
 BT94.C17 1990
 231.7'2—dc20   90–37621
                                            CIP

Printed in the United States of America

349 LB 9 8 7 6 5 4

To Joey Paul

A model for all of us who are trying to figure out what being a faithful husband and a good father really means.

. . . behold, the kingdom of God is within you.

Luke 17:21

Contents

Preface

A few years ago, I wrote a book that got me in a lot of trouble. The book, *A Reasonable Faith,* was by no means heretical; but it seemed as though some people consider it heresy if an attempt is made to express eternal truths in new ways. My book upset them. These good but staid critics believed not only that truth is sacred, but also that certain ways of expressing truth are sacred, too. For such people, there are verbal images which, instead of being viewed as vessels that carry the truth, are perceived as the truth itself. Thus, any attempt to give expression to the message of God through words or symbols that are not familiar to them is met with great resistance.

I believe that if we are to be faithful to the Great Commission and declare the gospel to all people at all times we must constantly be looking for ways to *contextualize* the message. That means putting the truth of God into words that people in a given place and time can relate to and understand.

Recently, a well-meaning Christian printed up tens of thousands of copies of a sermon preached by one of our Puritan ancestors. The sermon, "Sinners in the Hands of an Angry God," had been preached in a bygone century by Jonathan Edwards. It was a great sermon when it was produced many years ago, and I must admit that I still was able to get a great deal out of it when I read it. But today that sermon does not have the dynamic effect it had on people many years ago. The words, images, and style of the sermon belong to another place and another time. The message no longer has a cutting edge for most readers in our modern age. It just does not "connect," as they say.

Few, if any, books other than the Bible are able to relate to everybody, everywhere at any time. Therefore, writings that are less than the verbally inspired Scriptures have a temporality about them that limits their use. New attempts must always be made by those who seek to interpret the Bible through writings and speaking. Christian writers and speakers must search out new ways to say what they believe ought to be said, in words that stir and strike the people of this age.

This little volume is an attempt to do that. I want to say something of the truth of the Scriptures in a way that communicates to those who live in our technologically advanced societies of the Western world. The thoughts and the images I use to express my thoughts and beliefs come straight out of the Holy Writ. However, the biblical images I use are employed in ways that may seem new to some readers—and even a bit offensive to others. To the latter I can only say that no offense was intended. All I have tried to do is to tell the old, old story of the gospel from a somewhat new perspective. Feel free to criticize. But, if it comes to judgments—give me a break.

When it comes to writing books, I have come to depend on two people. First, there is my friend and associate, Mary Noel Keough. She is the one who types my writings, keeps them in order, corrects many errors, and gets everything off to my publisher. The other is my wife, Peggy, who is a brilliant editor and a superb critic. Without their help, this book would not have been written.

Chapter 1

A PARTY

IN HONOLULU

Whenever writers tell stories they are asked, "Did that really happen? Is that story really true?" Well, in this case, not entirely. While what I am about to describe really did happen, it did not happen in just the way I am going to tell it to you. The names and the setting are made up and dialogue is a bit contrived, but the story is essentially what happened to me about four years ago.

I do a lot of public speaking and my work takes me to all kinds of places. Some of them are exotic and some of them are not so exotic. Sometimes I get Honolulu and sometimes Toledo, Ohio.

If you live on the East Coast and travel to Hawaii, you know that there is a time difference that makes three o'clock in the morning feel like it's nine. If you know of what I speak, you will understand when I tell you that whenever I go out to our fiftieth state I find

4

myself wide awake long before dawn. Not only do I find myself up and ready to go while almost everybody else is still asleep, but I find that I want breakfast when almost everything on the island is still closed. With this background you should understand why at 3:30 in the morning I was wandering up and down the streets of Honolulu looking for a place to get something to eat.

Up a side street I found a little place that was still open. I went in, took a seat on one of the stools at the counter, and waited to be served. This was one of those sleazy places that deserves the name, "greasy spoon." I mean I did not even touch the menu. I was afraid that if I opened the thing something gruesome would crawl out. But it was the only place I could find.

The fat guy behind the counter came over and asked me, "What d'ya want?"

I told him. I said I wanted a cup of coffee and a donut.

He poured a cup of coffee, wiped his grimy hand on his smudged apron, and then he grabbed a donut off the shelf behind him. I'm a realist. I know that in the back room of that restaurant, donuts are probably dropped on the floor and kicked around. But when everything is out front where I could see it, I really would have appreciated it if he had used a pair of tongs and placed the donut on some wax paper.

As I sat there munching on my donut and sipping my coffee at 3:30 in the morning the door of the diner suddenly swung open and, to my discomfort, in marched eight or nine provocative and boisterous prostitutes.

It was a small place and they sat on either side of me. Their talk was loud and crude. I felt completely out of place and was just about to make my getaway when I overheard the woman sitting beside me say, "Tomorrow's my birthday. I'm going to be thirty-nine."

Her "friend" responded in a nasty tone, "So what do you want from me? A birthday party? What do you want? Ya want me to get you a cake and sing 'Happy Birthday'?"

"Come on!" said the woman sitting next to me. "Why do you have to be so mean? I was just telling you, that's all. Why do you have to put me down? I was just telling you it was my birthday. I don't want anything from you. I mean, why should you give me a birthday party? I've never had a birthday party in my whole life. Why should I have one now?"

When I heard that, I made a decision. I sat and waited until the women had left. Then I called over the fat guy behind the counter and I asked him, "Do they come in here every night?"

"Yeah!" he answered.

"The one right next to me, does she come here every night?"

"Yeah!" he said. "That's Agnes. Yeah, she comes in here every night. Why d'ya wanta know?"

"Because I heard her say that tomorrow is her birthday," I told him. "What do you say you and I do something about that? What do you think about us throwing a birthday party for her—right here—tomorrow night?"

A cute smile slowly crossed his chubby cheeks and he answered with measured delight, "That's great! I like it! That's a great idea!" Calling to his wife, who did the cooking in the back room, he shouted, "Hey! Come out here! This guy's got a great idea. Tomorrow's Agnes's birthday. This guy wants us to go in with him and throw a birthday party for her—right here—tomorrow night!"

His wife came out of the back room all bright and smiley. She said, "That's wonderful! You know Agnes is one of those people who is really nice and kind, and nobody ever does anything nice and kind for her."

"Look," I told them, "if it's O.K. with you, I'll get back here tomorrow morning about 2:30 and decorate the place. I'll even get a birthday cake!"

"No way," said Harry (that was his name). "The birthday cake's my thing. I'll make the cake."

At 2:30 the next morning, I was back at the diner. I had picked up some crepe-paper decorations at the store and had made a sign out of big pieces of cardboard that read, "Happy Birthday, Agnes!" I decorated the diner from one end to the other. I had that diner looking good.

The woman who did the cooking must have gotten the word out on the street, because by 3:15 every prostitute in Honolulu was in the place. It was wall-to-wall prostitutes . . . and me!

At 3:30 on the dot, the door of the diner swung open and in came Agnes and her friend. I had everybody ready (after all, I was kind of the M.C. of the affair) and when they came in we all screamed, "Happy birthday!"

Never have I seen a person so flabbergasted . . . so stunned . . . so shaken. Her mouth fell open. Her legs seemed to buckle a bit. Her friend grabbed her arm to steady her. As she was led to sit on one of the stools along the counter we all sang "Happy Birthday" to her. As we came to the end of our singing with "happy birthday dear Agnes, happy birthday to you," her eyes moistened. Then, when the birthday cake with all the candles on it was carried out, she lost it and just openly cried.

Harry gruffly mumbled, "Blow out the candles, Agnes! Come on! Blow out the candles! If you don't blow out the candles, I'm gonna hafta blow out the candles." And, after an endless few seconds, he did. Then he handed her a knife and told her, "Cut the cake, Agnes. Yo, Agnes, we all want some cake."

Agnes looked down at the cake. Then without taking her eyes off it, she slowly and softly said, "Look, Harry, is it all right with you if I . . . I mean is it O.K. if I kind of . . . what I want to ask you is . . . is it O.K. if I keep the cake a little while? I mean is it all right if we don't eat it right away?"

Harry shrugged and answered, "Sure! It's O.K. If you want to keep the cake, keep the cake. Take it home if you want to."

"Can I?" she asked. Then, looking at me she said, "I live just down the street a couple of doors. I want to take the cake home, O.K.? I'll be right back. Honest!"

She got off the stool, picked up the cake, and, carrying it like it was the Holy Grail, walked slowly toward the door. As we all just stood there motionless, she left.

When the door closed there was a stunned silence in the place. Not knowing what else to do, I broke the silence by saying, "What do you say we pray?"

Looking back on it now it seems more than strange for a sociologist to be leading a prayer meeting with a bunch of prostitutes in a diner in Honolulu at 3:30 in the morning. But then it just felt like the right thing to do. I prayed for Agnes. I prayed for her salvation. I prayed that her life would be changed and that God would be good to her.

When I finished, Harry leaned over the counter and with a trace of hostility in his voice, he said "Hey! You never told me you were a preacher. What kind of church do you belong to?"

In one of those moments when just the right words came, I answered, "I belong to a church that throws birthday parties for whores at 3:30 in the morning."

Harry waited a moment and then almost sneered as he answered, "No you don't. There's no church like that. If there was, I'd join it. I'd join a church like that!"

Wouldn't we all? Wouldn't we all love to join a church that throws birthday parties for whores at 3:30 in the morning?

Well, that's the kind of church that Jesus came to create! I don't know where we got the other one that's so prim and proper. But anybody who reads the New Testament will discover a Jesus who loved to party with whores and with all kinds of left-out people. The publicans and "sinners" loved Him because He partied with them. The lepers of society found in Him someone who would eat and drink with them. And while the solemnly pious could not relate to what He was about, those lonely people who usually didn't get invited to parties took to Him with excitement.

Our Jesus was and is the Lord of the party. This book is an attempt to make that point blatantly clear. It is an attempt to highlight an often-forgotten dimension of what Christianity is all about: The Kingdom of God is a party!

Chapter 2

SIGNS OF
THE KINGDOM

In our attempts to communicate the gospel, we are always looking for new words and images. What we have to say to the world is so expansive and rapturous that the linguistic tools available to us in our everyday conversations leave us with a sense of frustration. We know that God is doing something stupendous in us. We know that He is changing the world through us. And we know that the people of the world must be made to understand these things if they are to participate in bringing in those wonderful changes that God wills for all of humanity.

In the early part of this century, those Christian leaders known as the Social Gospelers made use of the biblical phrase, "Kingdom of God." These champions for social justice, including such notable preachers and activists as Walter Raushenbusch and Shailer Mathews, worked hard to communicate the idea that the salvation of God was much more than a way of getting people into heaven when they died; it was something to be experienced in this world. To them, salvation was something that not only transformed individuals; it was also something that transformed societies. They tried to tell church people that God had not saved them from sin solely for the purpose of granting them heavenly bliss, but in order to have a people who would work on earth for Him. Through those who become God's people, they said, God wills to change the institutions of society so that they do good and deliver justice. The Social Gospelers preached that God wills to be at work through His people transforming this world into the Kingdom of God.

In the Kingdom, all people will live out the life God planned for them when He first created the human race. In the Kingdom, family life, economic life, and political life will be lived out in accord with the plan of God. The Kingdom of God will be a society in which all people acknowledge God as King and relate to each other in ways prescribed by His love. This reconstructed world marked by justice will be a world in which evil will be vanquished, poverty will be eliminated, and war will be no more.

This image was biblical and it was powerful. All through the Hebraic scriptures and tradition there is a longing for the Kingdom. The message of Jesus was a declaration that this Kingdom was at hand. His parables were explanations of the Kingdom and His miracles were signs of the presence of God's Kingdom already present in the world.

When the propagators of the Social Gospel picked up this image they found a means to emphasize some dimensions of the gospel that the church had tended to ignore. However, in their zeal to emphasize the imperatives to change the institutions of society into structures that expressed love and justice, they overdid it. Their message of a God who wills to establish His Kingdom within human history deemphasized personal salvation. The Social Gospelers often passed over the fact that human beings as individuals are radically sinful and are in need of becoming new persons through a miracle of God.

The Social Gospelers became caught up by the hyper-optimism that characterized the attitude of the American people in the early 1900s and assumed that, as H. Richard Niebuhr has said: "A God without wrath brought men without sin into a Kingdom without judgment through the ministrations of a Christ without a cross." It remained for the fundamentalists to remind people that, as individuals, they needed to be "saved" from sin and transformed into new creatures through the power of the Holy Spirit.

THE CONCEPT OF SHALOM

During the 1950s, another biblical symbol or image came to the fore, as Christian leaders tried to find some new way to express God's mission in the world and to explain that people like us are to have a part in it. Many main-denominational theologians, particularly those associated with the World Council of Churches, took hold of the concept of *Shalom.* This old Hebrew word, which can simply be translated "peace," had a much deeper meaning in the ancient world than it did in the fifties, and an effort was made to recover that original meaning.

The Jews in Bible days used the word shalom when they greeted each other upon meeting, and as a fond farewell when they parted. To the Jews, the word shalom meant a time in which all people would live together as brothers and sisters, a time when no one would be hungry, and everyone would have "enough" to live life to the fullest. *Shalom* meant prosperity. It meant living in the land that flowed with milk and honey, where justice rolled down like the waters. Shalom was that time when the lion and the lamb would lie down together, swords would be reshaped into plowshares, and war would be no more. Shalom was the "this-world" hope for the people of Israel. It was the world that the Messiah would bring when He came.

The imagery provided by the word Shalom became a motif around which church leaders organized their activities. Building houses for poor people was done to contribute to Shalom. Fighting racism, supporting the peace movement, participating in efforts to save the environment—all were done to foster Shalom.

UNOBSERVED JUBILEE

Over the last few years, several neo-evangelical writers have made use of still another word to give expression to what they believe to be the purpose of the Christian mission. They have used the term "Jubilee." This symbol is especially useful for those who believe that the church should have a primary commitment to meet the needs of the poor and the oppressed. Writers such as Ron Sider and John Howard Yoder have made good use of the concept of Jubilee in their writings, as they have called Christians to a more responsible and simple lifestyle, so that resources might be available to minister to those who are without the food and shelter essential for survival.

The term Jubilee comes out of the writings of Moses. In Leviticus 25, we are told that God's law requires some special days and years to be set aside to honor Him as well as to contribute to our own good. Everyone is aware of the fact that God requires His people to observe a sabbath day each week. No reading of the Ten Commandments would leave us ignorant of that directive. What is less well known is that the Jews were also required to recognize a sabbatical year. The farmer was expected to divide up his land into seven sections and to allow one of the seven pieces to lie fallow each year. Thus, the land was given a chance for revitalization and renewal. It is from this requirement of scripture set forth in Leviticus 25:1–7 that those of us in academia have come up with the idea of a sabbatical leave every seven years.

But there was also a third requirement of the law of God in relation to the concept of the sabbath. And that was the commandment to observe Jubilee. According to Leviticus 25:8ff., on the fiftieth year there was to be a special observance in which, among other things, economic equity and justice were affirmed. All debts were to be canceled in the year of Jubilee. All land was to be returned to its original owners, and those who were in prison were to be set free. In those days, prison was primarily for debtors, since most other crimes were punishable by death.

Obviously, as the Bible says, Jubilee was good news for the poor. I can imagine how recent college graduates would react if it were suddenly announced that next year all debts incurred by education loans would be canceled. In the case of the truly poor in the ancient world, the cancellation of debts could mean deliverance from debtors' prison or from slavery. To the truly poor, Jubilee could be a whole new lease on life.

It is not surprising to learn that, so far as biblical historians can ascertain, the Jews never observed the year of Jubilee. There were various rationalizations and justifications for this nonobservance given by the rabbis, but the truth of the matter is that the Jews never fulfilled the complete law of the sabbath.

In the writings of the prophet Isaiah we learn that the fulfillment of the law of Moses with respect to the year of Jubilee would remain as something that the Messiah would do. According to Isaiah 61, we are told that when the Messiah comes, He will bring in the new economic order in which the poor will be delivered from all oppression and freed to live life to the fullest.

> The Spirit of the Lord God is upon me; because the Lord hath anointed me to preach good tidings unto the meek; he hath sent me to bind up the brokenhearted, to proclaim liberty to the captives, and the opening of the prison to them that are bound; To proclaim the acceptable year of the Lord, and the day of vengeance of our God; to comfort all that mourn. (Isa. 61:1–2)

Isaiah lets us know that, when the Messiah comes, we will know Him because He will declare this year "the year of the Lord" to Israel. This was to be the sign of His identity.

In light of this background, you can only guess what it must have been like on that day of worship in the synagogue at Nazareth when Mary's Son stood before a congregation of people and declared that the year of Jubilee was being instituted at His word.

The scene was set by the return of Jesus to His home town after having earned a significant reputation as a teacher and miracle worker down south in the region of Galilee. As was the custom in ancient Israel, visiting rabbis were always given the honor of reading from the Scriptures as part of sabbath worship services in the synagogue. Undoubtedly, the privilege was particularly meaningful to Mary when it was given to Jesus. This was her chance to show off her boy, who had taken such good care of the family following Joseph's death.

When they called upon Jesus to read the Scriptures, He asked for the scroll that contained the writings of Isaiah, turned to the passage cited above, and read it. Then He took His seat, even as every eye in the place was fixed on Him. What followed was the real shocker. Jesus shot back over His shoulder this incredible announcement: "This day is this scripture fulfilled in your ears" (Luke 4:21).

Nothing could have been more dramatic than the announcement that He deemed Himself to be the Messiah sent from God. Nothing could have been a more clear declaration that He saw Himself as the fulfillment of the prophecy made by Isaiah.

The crowd was faced with a decision. Either Mary's boy was the One sent from God, or He had just committed blasphemy. They decided that the latter was the case, and they took Jesus out to the edge of town to throw Him over a cliff.

What followed was awesomely dramatic by virtue of its simplicity. The Son of God did not call down an army of angels or suddenly disappear. Instead, in a scene that would make John Wayne seem like a sissy by comparison, Jesus turned on them and walked at the crowd. There must have been something powerful about His bearing, because the crowd that had been bent on killing Him simply stepped aside and let Him go without so much as laying a hand on Him (Luke 4:29–30).

The importance of all of this for us is that, in this act, Jesus made the declaration of Jubilee central to His mission and His identity. His salvation includes not only deliverance from sin and physical healings; it also involves a gift of economic well-being for the poor and downtrodden of the world. It is easy to see that this particular image of the work of Christ has special appeal to those who are trying to awaken contemporary Christians to the call of God to serve the poor and socially disinherited peoples of the world.

The main problem with this image, or symbol of the Christian mission, is that Jubilee, like the concept of *Shalom*, requires too much explanation to hammer home its meaning to most people. The emotions and social connotations that it is supposed to communicate are not self-evident. Something that will give a more immediate picture of what God wants to do in this world is needed. I have been groping for a word or image that can do that for us. And while no word or image can do the job as well as it should be done, I want to try out on you a word that I believe does communicate this description of God's Kingdom to the modern listener or reader. It is a word that conveys an immediate image to anyone who hears it. The word is "party." The Kingdom of God is a party. I hope you stay with me as I endeavor to make my case.

Chapter 3

IT'S PARTY
TIME

As I was reading Deuteronomy 14:22–29, the passage about tithing hit me hard. I realized that I had gotten it all wrong—I had always thought that what the Lord told Moses to tell us was to set aside 10 percent of all our earnings to give to the work of God (i.e., the ministries of the church). But as I read and re-read the passage, it was clear that the tithe was not for that at all. It was for partying.

A GIGANTIC CELEBRATION

Once a year, according to what Moses wrote in Deuteronomy 14, all the people of God were to bring one-tenth of all their earnings to the temple in Jerusalem. Imagine! One-tenth of Israel's GNP! And it was not to be used for mission work. It was not to be used for charity. It was not even to be used to build an education annex onto the temple. It was to be used on a gigantic party. Here! See for yourself:

> Thou shalt truly tithe all the increase of thy seed, that the field bringeth forth year by year. And thou shalt eat before the Lord thy God, in the place which he shall choose to place his name there, the tithe of thy corn, of thy wine, and of thine oil, and the firstlings of thy herds and of thy flocks; that thou mayest learn to fear the Lord thy God always.
>
> And if the way be too long for thee, so that thou art not able to carry it; or if the place be too far from thee, which the Lord thy God shall choose to set his name there, when the Lord thy God hath blessed thee: Then shalt thou turn it into money, and bind up the money in thine hand, and shalt go unto the place which the Lord thy God shall choose:
>
> And thou shalt bestow that money for whatsoever thy soul lusteth after, for oxen, or for sheep, or for wine, or for strong drink, or for whatsoever thy soul desireth: and thou shalt eat there before the Lord thy God, and thou shalt rejoice, thou, and thine household, And the Levite that is within thy gates; thou shalt not forsake him; for he hath no part nor inheritance with thee.
>
> At the end of three years thou shalt bring forth all the tithe of thine increase the same year, and shalt lay it up within thy gates: And the Levite, (because he hath no part nor inheritance with thee,) and the stranger, and the fatherless, and the widow, which are

within thy gates, shall come, and shall eat and be satisfied; that the Lord thy God may bless thee in all the
work of thine hand which thou doest. (Deut. 14:22–29)

No wonder little David could sing, "I was glad when
they said unto me, let us go unto the house of the
Lord." What kid wouldn't be thrilled to go to a gigantic
party? Not even a spoiled brat would have said "I don't
want to go! Church is boring!" Just look at that passage
of Scripture. The celebration on Mount Zion was anything but a bore. There was lots of food and plenty to
drink. There was dancing, singing, and exuberant celebration.

Everybody was invited to the party, from widows
who hadn't had a fun night out for a year, to poor
kids who couldn't have come up with ticket money to
whatever was the ancient equivalent of Disneyland.
Prostitutes and tax collectors were invited. So what if
their reputations were questionable? When it's a really
good party, you forget all that stuff. Everybody forgot
their titles and credentials at this wonderful party.
The rich danced with the poor. Management did a
"bottoms-up" with labor. The sophisticated intelli-
gentsia sang something like "Auld Lang Syne" with the
school dropouts. It was crazy!

If you are wondering what all this partying was
about, let me tell you. The party was, and is, about the
Kingdom of God. It has been planned by God to be a
foretaste of what He has in mind for all of us when His

Kingdom comes on earth as it is in heaven. Life may be hard. It may be full of troubles. But in the midst of it all, God tells us to set aside a tithe—a full 10 percent of all that we have earned through our labors—and to throw a party which will remind us of what God has in store for us.

The Scriptures tell us to spend all of this money for partying because it is in partying that we know a little something about the kind of God we have. He is not some kind of transcendental Shylock demanding His pound of flesh; He is not some kind of deistic chairperson of the universe. Our God is a party deity. He loves a party. If you don't believe me, then just pay attention to what His Son Jesus had to say about his Father's Kingdom.

> The kingdom of heaven is like unto a certain king, which made a marriage for his son, And sent forth his servants to call them that were bidden to the wedding: and they would not come. (Matt. 22:2–4)
> And he saith unto me, Write, Blessed are they which are called unto the marriage supper of the Lamb. And he saith unto me, These are the true sayings of God. (Rev. 19:9)

Did you get that? Jesus says the Kingdom is like a wedding reception and He wants His friends to celebrate with Him as though He were the bridegroom.

I have been to Jewish weddings. They are pretty much like Italian weddings. (And I know a lot about those!) With all of us Mediterranean types, wedding receptions are the ultimate blowout. I honestly believe you don't know what partying is all about until you've been to one of our wedding receptions. Parents mortgage their houses to get the money to do up the wedding in high style. They will go into debt if they have to. They will put every dollar they have on the line to make sure there is enough music and food and drink to keep everybody partying into the night! And Jesus said His Kingdom is like that!

Just the other day, I preached this good news about the Kingdom of God and a young couple "got me" as soon as I had finished. They let it be known in no uncertain terms that they found my message objectionable. They claimed that the Kingdom of God was marked by pain, suffering, and sacrifice, and that I was distorting the biblical message to say otherwise.

Of course I disagreed. This is not to say that Christians do not have to endure pain, suffering, and sacrifice. The history of Christianity makes clear that the saints of the church have had to endure all of these things. Christians follow a Christ who was a Man of sorrows, well acquainted with grief. Jesus carried a cross, and He warned all those who would dare to follow Him that they would have to do the same. But the reason our Lord and those who become His followers endure all this grief is to create the Kingdom. The pain, the suffering, and the sacrifice are all means to an end. And that end is the Kingdom of God.

I am quick to acknowledge that the Kingdom He declared is yet to come. The Kingdom of God with all its joyful celebration is still in the future. It will not fully come until a certain trumpet is sounded to herald the return of the Lord of the party, who then will preside over the festivities as the ultimate Master of Ceremonies. But what is to come is to be enjoyed now in part.

Whenever Christians party, they provide a foretaste of what is to come. Whenever they celebrate with laughter and song, they evangelize. They send out the message that the Kingdom of God is at hand—and the Kingdom of God is a wonderful party. It was this vision of what was to come that made it possible for Jesus to endure the agony of Calvary:

> Looking unto Jesus the author and finisher of our faith; who for the joy that was set before him endured the cross, despising the shame, and is set down at the right hand of the throne of God. (Heb. 12:2)

And it is the vision of what is coming that enables us to endure any suffering and pain that mark our present lives.

> The Spirit itself beareth witness with our spirit, that we are the children of God: And if children, then heirs; heirs of God, and joint-heirs with Christ; if so be that we suffer with him, that we may be also glorified

together. For I reckon that the sufferings of this present time are not worthy to be compared with the glory which shall be revealed in us. (Rom. 8:16–18)

For which cause we faint not; but though our outward man perish, yet the inward man is renewed day by day. For our light affliction, which is but for a moment, worketh for us a far more exceeding and eternal weight of glory; While we look not at the things which are seen, but at the things which are not seen; for the things which are seen are temporal; but the things which are not seen are eternal. (2 Cor. 4:16–18)

Our Jesus came that His joy might be in us and that our joy might be full (John 15:11).

Getting back to the passage of Scripture cited in the beginning of this chapter, let us once again look into the Old Testament concept of tithing. I have suggested that the 10 percent of each family's earnings which God ordered to be brought to the temple each year was not to be spent on missions or on typical "church projects." Instead, all of this money was to be spent on a good time that would give evidence of what kind of God we have and what kind of Kingdom He is building.

Please note! The tithe is a statement of how much we are supposed to spend on celebration. But the tithe also sets limits on what we are allowed to spend on partying. The other 90 percent of our earnings is to be used prayerfully in service to God, to family, and to those in need outside the family. The 90 percent is to be sanctified for the work God has called us to render as we join Him in establishing His Kingdom here on earth—as it is in Heaven (Matt. 6:10).

The thing that has gone wrong is obvious. We Christians, especially those of us who live in America, have turned the figures around. Instead of spending 10 percent on the party and 90 percent on Kingdom service, we usually end up spending 90 percent on partying and then, at best, set aside 10 percent for service in the missionary enterprise and to meet the needs of the poor.

The gospel is the good news about the celebration and partying that mark the Kingdom of God and, in the lives of Christians, that celebration and partying should already be evident. But, until the Kingdom comes in its fullness, there is work to be done. There is a message to be preached. There are miles to go. Between now and that glorious "then," we are still to party, but there are limits on how much we can spend on partying. That limit is 10 percent.

EMBARRASSED BY JESUS

I realize that for many Christians this emphasis on the Kingdom of God as being "a party" may seem inappropriate, and in some cases, a bit embarrassing. But then Jesus has always been a bit of an embarrassment to the piously religious. I recently came upon a newspaper item that made just this point. A certain owner of a restaurant in a "dry" county in Georgia applied to the county commissioners for permission to serve wine to his dinner guests. The permission was denied, in spite of the argument by the restaurant owner that Jesus Himself drank wine.

"I know He did," responded one of the commissioners, who also happened to be a Baptist deacon. "And He's always been an embarrassment to me because of that!"

Please! Do not get the idea that I am trying to justify booze. I simply want to drive home the point that our Jesus often leaves us a bit embarrassed by what He does and how He calls us to live. Even John the Baptist had trouble accepting some of the antics of Jesus. But remember that He said to all of us: "Blessed is he, whosoever shall not be offended in me" (Matt. 11:6).

Many of the Pharisees were among those who found Jesus an embarrassment to their preconceived images of what religion was all about. They were convinced that His partying lifestyle was a contradiction to what they considered to be marks of true spirituality.

Of course those pharisaical critics of Jesus were then, as they are now, people who can find fault, no matter what. Whenever our lifestyle is defined by the canons of "the religious" rather than by Scripture and the leading of the Spirit, we will find that "they" are impossible to please, no matter what we do. Jesus made a point of this when He responded to the criticisms leveled at Him by saying:

But whereunto shall I liken this generation? It is like unto children sitting in the markets, and calling unto their fellows, And saying, We have piped unto you, and ye have not danced; we have mourned unto you, and ye have not lamented. For John came neither eating nor drinking, and they say, He hath a devil. The Son of Man came eating and drinking, and they say, Behold a man gluttonous, and a winebibber, a friend of publicans and sinners. But wisdom is justified of her children. (Matt. 11:16–19)

In other words, Jesus was telling them that they were the kind of religious types who would not be satisfied, no matter what He did. Jesus let us know that, whatever lifestyle we adopt, there will be religious faultfinders who will pick us apart.

Judas was one of those judgmental types who had trouble with the partying dimensions of the lifestyle of Jesus. We read in John 12:1–8 how Mary, the sister of Lazarus, did one of those spontaneous things that make parties extra special. While Jesus and His friends were enjoying a great get-together, she slipped up to the Lord and poured some really expensive perfume over His feet. (It was probably worth about a thousand dollars.) That is not the sort of thing that would thrill anybody at one of our present-day parties, but it just goes to show how things can change. In ancient Israel, such an act was the kind of extravagant thing that drew "ohs" and "ahs" from people.

Evidently what Mary did told Jesus that He was the biggest thing in her life, and that she absolutely adored Him. But no sooner had she stunned everybody present with her joyful spontaneity, than old Judas spoke up and reminded all present that the perfume could have been sold and the money given to the poor. The old "killjoy" tried to throw cold water on the party; but our Jesus just would not let him get away with it. Instead, Jesus lauded what Mary had done and declared that wherever the gospel would be preached, the story of her gloriously extravagant expression of love would be told.

Ever since that time, there have been Pharisees and Judases who cannot let us enjoy ourselves without making snide remarks about the more utilitarian things that might have been done with the money spent on partying. We always must remind these phonies that our God loves us to party and even commands that we spend 10 percent of all our income (and I say it is "before taxes") on such seeming frivolities. When we go to Disneyland and enjoy the rides, our laughter is a taste of what God has in store for us. When we buy chocolate sundaes, we are getting something that will give us a taste of the good things planned for us in the Kingdom.

Ten percent of our income is to be spent on celebration. And when the Judases of the world give us pious reminders that the money could have been given to the needy, we ought to tell them that our God never planned for fun and celebration to be crowded out of our lives. In fact, the tithe was designated to pay for just these kinds of good times. To those who are upset with the declaration that the Kingdom of God is a party I would offer this reminder: Jesus performed His first miracle at a wedding reception (John 2:1–11). When it looked like the host was running out of wine, Jesus turned some water into wine, just to keep the party going. Praise be to God!

Chapter 4

WHOSOEVER WILL
MAY COME

John Carlson, a young Lutheran minister in Minnesota, gained attention and praise when he came up with the innovative idea that there should be a special party the night of the senior prom for those who did not have dates. All across America the night of the senior prom is a time of hurt feelings and deep depression for hundreds of thousands of high school kids. Not to have a date for the senior prom is to be publicly declared a reject. Everybody knows that those who can't get dates for the prom have to be losers. What is even sadder is that the sense of rejection and inferiority symbolized by being dateless on prom night has haunted these kids all through their school years. The prom simply provides the finishing blow.

So far as John Carlson was concerned, the prom was not the kind of party that Jesus would have liked. It was too exclusive to be Christian, in his opinion. It seemed to be reserved for the beautiful and the popular. So John planned an alternative to the prom for those whom "the system" had deemed losers and rejects. He called it the Reject Prom. Those who did not have dates were especially invited—and the kids loved it. The Reject Prom was held the same night as the senior prom and it turned out to be a real blowout party that made the senior prom seem tame and dull by comparison.

Once the thing got started, there was no stopping it. Each year the number attending this party for rejects grew. The party began to get press coverage. Timex Corporation gave watches to the kids who attended. Other companies joined in, and those who came to the Reject Prom were overwhelmed with interesting gifts and souvenirs. It wasn't long before some of the kids who could get dates and go to the prom decided not to. They preferred to join in the good time that the "rejects" were having at their special party.

What a great sign that the Kingdom of God is among us. What John Carlson pulled off must have had the angels in heaven chuckling and our Lord smiling. It is just the kind of celebration that He ordered in Deuteronomy 14:22–28. In that Old Testament party there were special orders to make the widows, the orphans, the crippled, and the blind the guests of honor. The Passover celebration was a party for those who couldn't afford one.

In the New Testament, the party is good news for the poor and the oppressed. The apostle Paul tells us that the big shots and the elite seldom show up for God's party. Instead it is the "rejects" who come.

> For ye see your calling, brethren, how that not many wise men after the flesh, not many mighty, not many noble, are called: But God hath chosen the foolish things of the world to confound the wise; and God hath chosen the weak things of the world to confound the things which are mighty. (1 Cor. 1:26–28)

Jesus faced the same prospect when He described His Kingdom.

> Then said he unto him, A certain man made a great supper, and bade many: And sent his servant at supper time to say to them that were bidden, Come; for all things are now ready. And they all with one consent began to make excuse. The first said unto him, I have bought a piece of ground, and I must needs go and see it: I pray thee have me excused. And another said, I have bought five yoke of oxen, and I go to prove them: I pray thee have me excused. And another said, I have married a wife, and therefore I cannot come. So that servant came, and shewed his lord these things. Then the master of the house being angry said to his servant, Go out quickly into the streets and lanes of the city, and bring in hither the poor, and the maimed, and the halt, and the blind. And the servant said, Lord, it is done as thou hast commanded, and yet there is room. And the lord said unto the servant, Go out into the

highways and hedges, and compel them to come in, that my house may be filled. (Luke 14:16–23)

The rich and powerful are too busy to come. But blessed are the poor. They're not too busy to show up.

A PARTY FOR EVERYONE

A real tragedy of our world is that so many people seem to be shut out of God's party. This is not God's will. He wants His party to be inclusive and it grieves Him for it to be otherwise.

A few years ago a man called my office with a very unusual request. Knowing that I head up a missionary organization that has a variety of programs in Haiti, he wondered if it were possible to go to a village in Haiti and throw a Christmas dinner for everybody who lived there. He envisioned a couple of hundred people on Christmas Day having turkey, sweet potatoes, cranberry sauce—the whole typical North American spread.

To tell the truth, I thought the idea was crazy when he first approached me with it. But the more I thought about it, the more I saw it as a positive possibility. Of course the usual questions of whether or not it was proper for people of one culture to impose their particular forms of celebration on the people of another culture came to my mind. But knowing the poverty of the people in Haiti, I came to the conclusion that a typically North American meal would be better than going hungry on Christmas Day.

I forwarded the money the man provided for the feast to the Haitian pastor who directs some of the ministries which we support, and he made all the necessary arrangements. On Christmas Day, the village people welcomed their North American benefactor and his family and together they had a party.

It was great. The joy and celebration that marked the feast were mind-boggling. The infectious laughter of children, the singing of teen-agers, the smiles on the faces of adults, all combined to make the party the best one anybody could remember. Undoubtedly, it was the best party this man ever went to, and it was the best Christmas he and his family ever enjoyed.

The honored guests at that party in Haiti were the poor and the oppressed. That is the kind of party that pleases the Lord—the kind He prescribed in Deuteronomy 14.

If our Lord's Kingdom is comprised of people who can joyfully celebrate the goodness of life which He has ordained, then we must see to it that nobody is prevented from enjoying the party. If ghetto kids in Philadelphia have little to celebrate because they have hovels for homes and live in the midst of gang violence, then we must do something to change all of that. If blacks in South Africa have to endure humiliation because of apartheid, then apartheid must be destroyed. If the Palestinians are denied human rights and are made into aliens in the very land in which they were born, then we must protest. If Catholics in Northern Ireland are made into second-class citizens by the Protestant majority, then we must work and pray for the restructuring of the Irish social system.

In simple words, we must be committed to destroying all of those barriers that keep our brothers and sisters from entering into the celebration of life which is the mark of the Kingdom of God. It is our calling to join with Christ to destroy all of those works of the devil (1 John 3:7–10).

Sitting in front of a television set in a hotel in Zurich, Switzerland, I was between airplanes on my way home from Africa. Feelings of loneliness and anxiousness about getting home were keeping me from sleeping. Then, onto the TV screen came pictures of the closing celebration of the Olympic games. At first, the teams, wearing their official uniforms and carrying their national flags, marched around the stadium in a structured parade that looked like soldiers on review.

Then suddenly the Olympians broke ranks. They ran and danced with one another in a spontaneous outpouring of enthusiasm. The neat columns were gone. Nationalistic identities were destroyed. There were no longer winners and losers, communists and capitalists, whites and blacks, Hispanics and Asians, rich and poor. There were only happy, dancing people hugging each other and loving each other. In that ecstatic moment, all divisions between humanity were wiped out. In a split second, the socially created barriers between the peoples of the world were forgotten. All at once there was joyful pandemonium and unspeakable joy.

As I watched that faraway party, my depression disappeared. Even though I was all alone, I stood up and applauded. And as I cheered, I sensed God saying to me that this is what it was like on the day of Pentecost and this is what it will be like when the Kingdom comes in its fullness.

From the book of Acts we read:

And when the day of Pentecost was fully come, they were all with one accord in one place. And suddenly there came a sound from heaven as of a rushing mighty wind, and it filled all the house where they were sitting. And there appeared unto them cloven tongues like as of fire, and it sat upon each of them. And they were all filled with the Holy Ghost, and began to speak with other tongues, as the Spirit gave them utterance.

And there were dwelling at Jerusalem Jews, devout men, out of every nation under heaven. Now when this was noised abroad, the multitude came together, and were confounded, because that every man heard them speak in his own language.

And they were all amazed and marvelled, saying one to another, Behold, are not all these which speak Galilaeans? And how hear we every man in our own tongue, wherein we were born? Parthians, and Medes, and Elamites, and the dwellers in Mesopotamia, and in Judaea, and Cappadocia, in Pontus, and Asia, Phrygia, and Pamphylia, in Egypt, and in the parts of Libya about Cyrene, and strangers of Rome, Jews and proselytes, Cretes and Arabians, we do hear them speak in our tongues the wonderful works of God.

And they were all amazed, and were in doubt, saying one to another, What meaneth this? (2:1–12)

In the party generated by the Holy Spirit, all divisions are obliterated: "There is neither Jew nor Greek, there is neither bond nor free, there is neither male nor female: for ye are all one in Christ Jesus" (Gal. 3:28).

As I watched that TV scene, I saw the vision—through a glass darkly—of the party that gave birth to the church and the party that will mark the eventual triumph of the church in that moment. What I saw only made me long for that day when I will see it face to face. The vision of what will be stirred within me incredible dissatisfaction with what actually is right now.

The party that is to come makes me unwilling to tolerate all systems and structures that keep the party from happening now. There is nothing that fosters social change like a tiny glimpse of the party that will be given by the God who promises it to us by His grace.

A Party of Peace

Sociologists long have known that radical social change and revolution do not occur because things are deplorable as much as they occur when people see the possibilities of what could be. Little tastes of the party God has in store for us make me want to destroy the unjust social arrangements in this world that keep the party called "God's Kingdom" from being realized. The foretaste of party is a prelude to God's revolution. That image of the Kingdom of God at the Los Angeles Olympics was something I must remember.

> But as it is written, Eye hath not seen, nor ear heard, neither have entered into the heart of man, the things which God hath prepared for them that love him. (1 Cor. 2:9)

What sociologists do not know is how powerful a force for peace a party can be. During the Civil War, the army of the Union and the army of the Confederacy were locked in a vicious battle to the death just outside the city of Richmond. As night fell after the first day of the battle, cheers were heard from the Confederate lines. When General Grant asked what was going on behind the enemy's line, he was told that the wife of General George Pickett had given birth to a baby boy, and that his troops were celebrating.

Upon receiving the news, General Grant ordered bonfires to be lit and a toast to be given. Cheers and hoorahs rang out all night long. For a few hours, the shooting stopped and warring soldiers were drawn together for a birthday party. The birth of Pickett's son only temporarily stopped a war. But it stands as evidence of what a good birthday party can do.

The good news is that another Son was born, and there were some who stopped what they were doing and enjoyed a little bit of peace for just a little while. There was singing in the sky—at least some shepherds said there was. And some strange visitors came looking for a baby whom they nicknamed the Prince of Peace. Everyone has not gotten the message, so not everyone knows about the baby. But the baby started a movement and we know that someday everyone will come to His party and call Him the Lord of the feast.

There's a great day coming when the world will change. The lion will lie down with the lamb. Swords will be beaten into plowshares. And people will forget about war. What started as a birthday party will end with a wedding feast. We will call it the "Kingdom of God." We must pray for it, and we must work for it.

Chapter 5

COUNTERFEIT
PARTIES

Chapter 5

COUNTERFEIT
PARTIES

The world has its parties, too. And at first glance those parties seem more attractive than the party God is throwing. There is an abundance of glitz at the world's parties. They seem to be so glamorous and exciting. They seem to attract more interesting people. To be invited to the world's parties is often the best affirmation that you are "somebody," that you are desirable. The demonic powers at work in the world are almost always able to make these parties seem like the places to be.

The movie *Animal House* portrayed the college fraternity party as the best fun any late adolescent could hope to enjoy. With its star-studded cast, it made frat life out to be a blast and a half. The wit, cleverness, and "good-time" styles of Bill Mung and his frat brothers looked like ample insurance that the party time they were offering was absolutely the "in" thing to do during the college years.

In reality, the opposite is the case. On many university campuses, fraternities have been disbanded by administration officials because their parties have proven to be cruel, dehumanizing, and dangerous. At three of the universities in my home town of Philadelphia, action has been taken against fraternities because their brutalities at parties resulted in the deaths of students.

The feminists on most large university campuses have been outraged by fraternity parties because of what they have done to women. According to solid sociological studies, more than one-quarter of all university women report that they have been raped or have barely escaped attempted rapes. The overwhelming proportion of these rapes have been what is referred to as "date rapes." That means that the men attempting the rapes were fellow collegians who made the rape attempts a part of what they figured went along with a good date.

Campus feminists claim that among the more likely places for such goings-on are parties at fraternity houses. Just recently, at one of the Ivy League schools, a young woman was gang raped at a frat house, and the school did very little to discipline the men involved. After all, suggested the lawyer for the defendants, "it was just a situation in which some boys let partying get out of hand."

During my days of teaching at a large university, I got my fill of hearing about the debauchery of frat parties. I heard about the beer drinking that turned into vomiting, and on one occasion listened as some staggering-drunk, sick sophomores tried to tell me they were having a good time.

WHO NEEDS IT?

But let us turn from the most abusive college scenes and look in on the Christmas parties at the offices of some white-collar businesses. Consider what has become all too typical. At too many office parties, we find the same kind of drinking that goes on at frat parties. Often people make fools of themselves at office parties and have to spend weeks living down the behavioral displays that they call "celebrating."

One New Year's Eve, I answered my phone and heard the slurred speech of the anonymous person at the other end of the line mumbling, "Happy New Year!" When I asked who was speaking, the woman sadly cried, "Oh, God! What am I doing? What's wrong with me?" and hung up.

So many of the world's parties remind me of the little boy at Disneyland who was crying his eyes out while his mother was shaking him and shouting, "You wanted to come! And now you're going to have a good time whether you like it or not!" Or, more to the point, they seem to have too many guests who could echo the words of Søren Kierkegaard, the Danish existentialist philosopher who wrote in his diary:

Last night I went to a party. Everyone admired my wit and sophistication. All agreed that I was most entertaining. And I returned to my apartment, closed the door, held a gun in my hands and thought about blowing out my brains.

But we do not have to view the pain too often evident amid the world's parties through the eyes of an existentialist philosopher suffering from a severe case of angst in order to make negative judgments about them. Just take a look at that American party which many of us consider to be wholesome—namely, the school dance. I have been there and so have most of you. I have watched those scores of girls who sit on folding chairs that line the gym walls; they hurt because they are passed over for the prettier ones. I know what it is like to be an awkward, nervous boy who would love to ask a girl to dance—but won't for fear of rejection. And I have inwardly wept for the left-out ones who never even show up for these parties because they know what will happen to them.

Perhaps you, too, have been there and back. And like so many middle-aged people, you may say, "There are a lot of ages I would like to be again. But one thing is sure. I would not want to go back and be a teen-ager and have to go through that kind of thing again." It is no wonder to me that when I talk to teen-agers about these so-called "healthy" school activities, they cynically respond with, "Who needs it?" Who needs it, indeed?

THE GREAT AMERICAN PARTY

My friend, author Tom Sine, makes good use of the imagery of the party when he talks about the American way of life. He refers to the lifestyle that has become normative in this country as the "Great American Party." He points out that this party is very expensive. Sports cars, extravagant clothes, and fancy jewelry have become necessary accessories for those who want to attend.

People, he points out, often have to hold down a couple of jobs to have enough money to buy all the stuff our society says is essential if we are to enjoy ourselves. They sometimes spend so much time getting enough money to buy these things and take proper care of them that they haven't any time left to give to relationships with those who are nearest and dearest to them. These poor victims of "getting" have no time or energy for giving anything much to their children, their partners, or anyone else. These American party people end up missing out on what can really make life joyful and meaningful.

Tom, who for several years worked on a missionary project in Haiti, tells a story which contrasts the shallowness of many American parties with the richness of a party he shared in that poorest country of the Western hemisphere. On one of his trips to Haiti, Tom traveled with a young man who had been studying in the United States. This student was returning to his village along the southern peninsula of the country, and he invited Tom to come along. As they arrived at the remote community, literally everyone in the village ran out to greet them. They were all over the young man, hugging him, throwing him into the air and catching him, and patting him all over his head and back while giving him shouts and cheers of welcome.

As Tom watched the celebration of the poorest of the poor, in that village he sensed how much richer it was than most of the impoverished parties which rich suburbanites throw here in the wealthiest nation on the face of the earth. Those empty, insipid cocktail parties, so brilliantly exposed by the writings of T. S. Eliot, could never hold a candle to the joyful celebrations of the people of God when they get together to love one another in His name.

WHEN BABYLON FALLS

Undoubtedly, the most dramatic contrast between the party which is promoted by the world and the party thrown by the Lord comes to us from the book of Revelation. In the seventeenth chapter through the middle of the nineteenth chapter of this book, the apostle John contrasts the ways of this world, symbolized by the great whore of Babylon, with the glories of the Kingdom of God, symbolized by the New Jerusalem. In Revelation 17:3–4, we read about the glitzy allurements of the whore, who is the embodiment of all that is seductive about this world.

The whore, who is out to draw us to herself, defiles all who succumb to her ways.

> The merchandise of gold, and silver, and precious stones, and of pearls, and fine linen, and purple, and silk, and scarlet, and all thyine wood, and all manner vessels of ivory, and all manner vessels of most precious wood, and of brass, and iron, and marble, And cinnamon, and odours, and ointments, and frankincense, and wine, and oil, and fine flour, and wheat and beasts, and sheep, and horses, and chariots, and slaves, and souls of men.
>
> And the fruits that thy soul lusted after are departed from thee, and all things which were dainty and goodly are departed from thee, and thou shalt find them no more at all.
>
> The merchants of these things, which were made rich by her, shall stand afar off for the fear of her torment, weeping and wailing. . . . (Rev. 18:12–15)

As I read these passages, I think of how this country that I love has taken the natural resources of poorer countries and turned the land of Third World nations into the production of cash crops like sugar, tobacco, and coffee in order to feed the addictions of people like me. I think of how much blood has been shed under the oppressive heels of American-supported dictators so that multinational businesses can provide us with things to satisfy our artificially generated wants. The Great American Party, as Sine calls it, has been maintained at great expense to the poorer peoples of the world.

But God will not let the exploitation and the oppression continue indefinitely. He will stop it. Babylon will be brought down. And when it falls, there will be two reactions. First there will be the weeping and mourning of the business people who got rich on the commercial trade that fed the appetites of those who were identified with Babylon and the party of the great whore. Those dictators, whose power and wealth came from compliance with the whore and the destructive, luxurious lifestyle that went with her way of life, will be overwhelmed with grief and anxiety because their protectress is no more. We read of these reactions in Revelation 18:9–11.

> And the kings of the earth, who have committed fornication and lived deliciously with her, shall bewail her and lament for her, when they shall see the smoke of her burning, Standing afar off for the fear of her torment, saying, Alas, alas that great city Babylon, that mighty city! for in one hour is thy judgment come. And the merchants of the earth shall weep and mourn over her; for no man buyeth their merchandise any more.

But there is also a second reaction, and that is the reaction of the angels to the fall of Babylon (i.e., the

Great American Party). We read in the nineteenth chapter of Revelation:

> And after these things I heard a great voice of much people in heaven, saying, Alleluia; Salvation and glory, and honour, and power, unto the Lord our God: For true and righteous are his judgments: for he hath judged the great whore, which did corrupt the earth with her fornication, and hath avenged the blood of his servants at her hand. And again they said, Alleluia. And her smoke rose up for ever and ever. (vv. 1–3)

There is a party in heaven because the party that meant destruction for so many has been ended. A new celebration sponsored by God has gotten under way. According to this scripture, those allied with the Lamb of God cannot help but shout, "Hallelujah!" at this incredible turn of events.

WILL YOU FALL WITH BABYLON?

There are two questions to be asked about this interpretation of these passages from the closing chapters of the Bible. The first is probably a question you would like to ask of me. "Where did you come up with your particular interpretation of Scripture that makes the great whore of Babylon in the book of Revelation a symbol of the affluent lifestyle which Tom Sine calls the Great American Party?"

My response is to point out that many of the most credible biblical scholars have agreed that Babylon in the Book of Revelation always refers to the dominant society in which Christians have to live. For those in the first-century church, that dominant society was Rome. Thus, for those early Christians, Babylon was a code word for the Roman Empire, while Jerusalem was the code word for the Kingdom of God, which is composed of the people who identify with the Lord.

This being the case, Christians in every age will look upon the society in which they live, and all of its seductive allurements, as Babylon. To the English Christians in the nineteenth century, Babylon would be England. To the Japanese Christians in our contemporary world, it is Japan, and to those Christians who live in the Soviet Union, Babylon is the Soviet Union. But ours is the American society. The great party to which Tom Sine alludes is in our country. I love America. I believe it to be the best Babylon on the face of the earth. But it is still Babylon.

The second question is one that I direct at you, the reader. Quite simply, it is this: When our Babylon falls (and it, like all Babylons, will one day fall), how will you react? Will you react like the merchants described in Revelation 18:3 who "grew rich from her excessive luxuries" and those political potentates who conspired with her to exploit the weak and the poor? Or will you be able to join the angels on that day and sing praises to God?

Of course, the way you answer this second question has everything to do with how you have invested your life. Have you given your time and energy to get those things that go with living in Babylon so that, when it falls, all that you have ever worked for will fall with it? Or have you so invested your life in the Kingdom of God that, even if heaven and earth shall pass away, what is important to you will endure? In the end, will you be able to shout and sing in that eternal party that will be shared by those who have laid up their treasures in heaven (Matt. 6:19–21)?

Chapter 6

TURNING CHURCH
INTO A PARTY

When we realize that for the Passover the ancient Jews took one-tenth of their annual income to Jerusalem and blew it on a stupendous party, we can understand why their kids might all have said, "I was glad when they said unto me, let us go unto the house of the Lord." Who wouldn't want to go to the house of the Lord if it meant going to the biggest and best party imaginable? The Jews knew how to celebrate, and celebration was at the heart of their worship of God.

King David, the foremost of all their kings, set a pattern for worship by dancing before the Lord. After the blessings and victories which God had given Israel, David led his people in a dance that may well have been a combination of break dancing, the Charleston, and the bunny hop. Of course we don't know the details of all his moves and steps, but we do know that the king nearly danced out of his clothes.

Some of the young virgins at the celebration got a bit "turned on" by David's gyrations and this got David's wife Michal very upset. And she let David know how she felt in no uncertain terms. She considered his behavior disgraceful and evidently she was not one of those persons who kept her opinions private. The Scripture says:

> And as the ark of the Lord came into the city of David, Michal Saul's daughter looked through a window and saw King David leaping and dancing before the Lord; and she despised him in her heart. (2 Sam. 6:16)
> Then David returned to bless his household. And Michal the daughter of Saul came out to meet David, and said, How glorious was the king of Israel today, who uncovered himself today in the eyes of the handmaids of his servants, as one of the vain fellows shamelessly uncovereth himself! (2 Sam. 6:20)

Responding to the criticism with his own display of anger, David curses Michal for her prudish party-dampening attitude.

> And David said unto Michal, It was before the Lord, which chose me before thy father, and before all his house, to appoint me ruler over the people of the Lord, over Israel; therefore will I play before the Lord. And I will yet be more vile than thus, and will be base in mine own sight: and of the maidservants which thou has spoken of, of them shall I be had in honour.

Therefore Michal the daughter of Saul had no child unto the day of her death. (2 Sam. 6:21–23)

God's judgment was on this party pooper. Michal never did have any children and it was from the lineage of David and Bathsheba (yes, Bathsheba) that the Messiah was born. So much for those who put down partying as a form of worship.

When we come to the New Testament, we find that the same spirit of celebration is continued—only more so. On the Day of Pentecost, when the Holy Spirit came upon God's people and made them into a church, there were such carryings on that outsiders thought the Christians were drunk. The response of Peter to the accusation was classic:

But Peter, standing up with the eleven, lifted up his voice, and said unto them, Ye men of Judaea, and all ye that dwell at Jerusalem, be this known unto you, and hearken to my words: For these are not drunken, as ye suppose, seeing it is but the third hour of the day.

Peter didn't deny that they might look like a bunch of drunks with all their carrying on; instead he simply pleaded for the critics to realize that it was only nine in the morning and that people just don't drink themselves into that kind of frenzied state so early in the day.

I don't know what's happened to us since then. My colleagues in the field of sociology say that it is inevitable. Their argument is that over a period of time any social movement loses its exuberance and takes on a more rational form. As a matter of fact, Max Weber, one of the founders of sociology, referred to this process as "the routinization of charisma."

But the church is not supposed to be just any social movement. The church is supposed to be a living organism, a body of believers endowed with a heavenly dynamism; it is supposed to be the living body of Christ.

Something has gotten lost. Something has died. Something that was hot has become lukewarm. Something that is essential has to be renewed.

Make a Joyful Noise

Every year for the past ten years in central Pennsylvania, I have spoken at a big "Jesus festival" called Creation. To those who have never been to one of these Jesus festivals, the best I can do to describe them is to say that they are religious versions of Woodstock. About forty thousand people, mostly in their teens, camp out together for four days, groove on Christian rock music, listen to gospel preachers, and have an overall good time. The flavor of the get-together is somewhat reflective of neo-pentecostalism but not too much so. A few people get into speaking in tongues, but for the most part, it is the style of worship that gives evidence of being in the charismatic movement. Many people raise their hands while singing hymns and there are a lot of "hallelujahs" and "amens" during the preaching.

A couple of years ago, I was invited to preach at a Lutheran church in Lancaster, Pennsylvania, just a couple of days after the Creation festival ended. Lancaster is close to the site of the festival, and evidently, the word had gotten around to a lot of the people who attended the festival that I was preaching there. That Sunday evening, they showed up in large numbers and packed the place. I don't know what the pastor of the church made of the huge turnout for that Sunday evening service. I believe he was somewhat surprised that his publicity through the local papers had been so effective.

Dressed in his black robe with its velvet decorations, he took his place behind the pulpit. He opened the gilded pulpit Bible, stood back with a dignified flair and, unsuspecting of what was to follow, called the people to worship by saying,"Let us make a joyful noise unto the Lord! Let us come into His gates with thanksgiving and into His courts with praise!"

With that, someone in the balcony yelled, "All right! All right!" and stood up clapping. That outburst was followed by several hundred young people who followed suit by jumping to their feet with shouts of praise and wild applause.

The pastor was visibly startled. I do not know what he was expecting when he told the people in the church to make a joyful noise unto the Lord. But I do know that the last thing he expected that Sunday night was that anybody actually would!

I do not know what the regular church members thought of what went on during the unusual hour that followed. But one thing is for sure: They did not find it boring.

The fact that this particular church service was wildly exciting makes it exceptional. Because, generally, church services are devoid of excitement. Ask any teenager who doesn't want to go to church on a Sunday morning why, and you will get a standard answer: "Church is boring." They are not simply knocking the choir or the sermon. It is something else that they protest. It is the atmosphere of the place. It's too serious. There is a dull feeling. There is no sense that something spontaneously joyful is about to erupt. There is no electricity in the air. Certainly, going to church is nothing like going to a fun-packed party. And that's a shame.

At Sunday services in the Roman Catholic Church, they say that the priest is celebrating the Mass. The first time I heard that, I thought it was strange to put it that way. It seemed to me that the one thing that the somber man in the front of the altar was not doing was celebrating. But that is exactly what he was supposed to be doing. That is what the whole church of Jesus Christ is supposed to be doing when its people worship on Sunday morning. We are all supposed to be celebrating the resurrection of Jesus. Satan thought he had outsmarted God when Jesus got spiked to the cross. But God tricked Satan and surprised him with the resurrection.

In Russia, on Easter Sunday afternoon, the Orthodox priests used to get together to tell jokes. They would spend the afternoon hours getting each other to enjoy belly laughs as they told one-liners and tall tales. Resurrection Sunday was to be a time for joy and laughter. It was to be for celebration—and partying.

I do not want to communicate that every worship service must be a rambunctious show. I realize that such is easy to assume from everything I have said up to this point. But if that is the case, please reconsider. I honestly believe that there are other people with other temperaments and dispositions who find it difficult to handle my kind of party. They need parties that especially suit them.

DIFFERENT PARTIES FOR DIFFERENT PEOPLE

The Bible gives ample evidence that God has ordained for there to be different parties for different kinds of people. It gives special consideration to the special needs of individual ethnic groups. And there is a strong directive in Scripture for each ethnic group to worship God in its own particular way.

The word "nation" in the New Testament is the Greek word "ethnos," which actually means "ethnic group." It does not refer to the political entities we now refer to as nations, but, rather, it refers to particular races with their unique cultural characteristics. According to Scripture, each is supposed to actualize its own potentialities and give expression to its own genius. That means that Polish people will, on that day of the ultimate party, worship God in a distinctly Polish way. They will dance Polish dances before the Lord. They will sing Polish hymns of praise and celebration. And they will throw a Polish feast. So it will be with the Bavarians, and the Irish, and the Ukrainians, and the Cantonese, the Japanese, the Sicilians, the Celts, the Arabians, and the Persians. They all will be there, gathered around the throne of God. Among them will be numbered peoples and tribes whose names and identities have been lost in the surging parade of history. Parthians, Medes, Elamites, Phyrigians, and Pamphylians will all be there.

Once a year the people of Philadelphia get together for what they call Super Sunday. They come together by the tens of thousands. They gather on the Benjamin Franklin Parkway, a wide boulevard that was designed to be like the Champs-Elysées in Paris. Philadelphia is a multi-ethnic city, and on Super Sunday each of them sets up a stage and some booths at designated locations, and each group does its thing.

If you go to the Italian location, you will see Italian performers singing and dancing on stage. At the accompanying booths you will find Italian foods and pastries for sale. There will be Italian crafts on display and many people will be dressed in old-country Italian clothes.

The same scenario is played out at the Swedish location, as it is at the Turkish, the German, the Hispanic, and the African-American. Each ethnic group struts its stuff. Each shows off in the best kind of ethnic pride. I have a conviction that the great party which is to come will be like Super Sunday. I believe that every ethnic group of time and history will be there and that each will enjoy the others as they party together and with the Lord. I do not believe that ethnic identities are displaced in heaven, but rather are lifted up and glorified.

While I was sharing this imagery of the Kingdom of God with an audience in New Zealand, a young Maori tribesman gave special attention to my message. When the lecture was over, he came up to me and sadly told me that he was afraid that at that glorious party that is to come, he would not know which dance to dance or which songs to sing. He told me that he had danced the Pakeha dance (representing the English culture of New Zealand) so long that he might have forgotten how to dance the Maori dance or sing the Maori songs. This sad young man told me that he was going to make sure in the future that he relearned the dances, songs, and stories of his past so that he might be able to offer them up to God when the trumpet sounds, heralding the signal that the ultimate party is about to begin.

There was a period when missionaries were propagators not only of the gospel but of the Anglo culture as well. Authors such as Michener mocked this style of missionary work that made God into an Englishman and Christian worship into an acting out of the Anglican Book of Common Prayer. But that day has long since passed. Nowadays, most missionaries, informed by anthropologists, are cross-culturally sensitive and do their best to "contextualize" the gospel so that it is expressed in forms and words that are inherent in indigenous cultures.

Recently, Wycliffe Bible Translators, one of the largest and most effective missionary organizations in the world today, has come up for criticism by officials in the Brazilian government. It seems as though the Wycliffe Bible Translators have reduced the languages of various Amazon tribes to writing and then translated the Bible into these tribal languages. In so doing, they had provided impetus for these various tribes to preserve their tribal identities.

By putting not only the Bible into writing so that the tribes could read it, but also recording their folklore and tribal history the missionaries had lent support to the preservation of tribal identities that some in the Brazilian government would as soon see left behind and forgotten. There were officials in Brasilia who wanted the tribal cultures of the Amazon swallowed up into a new, modern Brazilian culture, and to them the Wycliffe missionaries seemed to be running counter to that purpose.

I laud those missionaries. I believe that in assisting in the revitalization of tribal cultures they were preparing various ethnic peoples to bring something special to that great party which we call the Kingdom of Heaven. What they were doing would enrich the eternal party for all of us.

It is my opinion that on the collective level there is a kind of personality to each and every ethnic group. Furthermore, I believe that redemption does not prescribe the obliteration of these 'societal personalities,' but the perfecting of them. Through the grace of God each ethnic group—and its unique traits—will be lifted up. Thus, in the end, the Maori people will not be less Maori, but more Maori than ever before. I am convinced that on that great day the Maori culture will be purged of all corrupting influences that have come both from sin and from other societies. In a purified form it will be presented as a gift to all other peoples and to the God who willed it into being.

This, I believe, will also be true of the Apache Indians, the Seminoles, the Naga tribe of Burma, and the Todas of India. All the traits of all the ethnic cultures which are contrary to the will of the God who created them (as wood, hay or straw) will be burned away so that each might be presented pure and spotless (as gold, silver and precious stones) before the heavenly Father (1 Cor. 3:12).

If part of who we really are is wrapped up in our ethnic identities, then we can never be wholly what we are supposed to be until we recover our true ethnicity at God's great party.

The church in today's world should reflect the glorious variety of ethnic peoples as described in Scripture. The church ought to give support and to encourage each ethnic group to be all that it can be and to challenge each to worship in its own way. The church, therefore, should be multicultural, allowing for each ethnic group to demonstrate something now that will be expressed in fullness on the coming day of glory.

Worship here in this world should be a dress rehearsal for what will happen there, when we are gathered together with God. Some will be there in African costumes and music, while others will provide an Asian flavor. But some will come with the likes of Handel's "Messiah" and the "Gloria Patri." Those whose parties are somewhat reserved by comparison need not become what they are not in order to fully qualify in this coming celebration. Each group is called to be what God created it to be; and to be otherwise will be to stand in judgment (and there *will* be a judgment of the nations, i.e., ethnic groups). It's a glorious kaleidoscope Church that is coming. And the Church of the present should evidence this.

GENERATING JOY

Music certainly helps to create a party atmosphere for church. In this respect, much of the new music coming out of the charismatic movement has blessed the entire Christian community. The contemporary praise music which picks up scriptural passages but also vibrates with modern rhythms has generated a whole new quality to worship. But we must always be aware that there is no one musical style that can be designated as "the" holy one. In reality, all kinds of music can be sacred.

What lifts the spirit for some people may be quite different than that which lifts the spirit for others. There are some for whom Christian rock is primary, while there are others who only get turned on by the classical music of Bach. However, if churches are to generate joy and celebration, there must be a willingness to experiment with various musical expressions and to innovate in the use of music in all parts of church life.

Festive banners have proven to be another useful means of livening up church sanctuaries. The teenagers in a certain church I know made it a project of their youth group to make banners with simple words like "celebrate," "rejoice," and "hallelujah." They hung these banners on every area of empty wall they could find. The effect was immediate. Worship became lively. People became spontaneous. Even the music and the sermons seemed to be more vibrant. The creation of a festive atmosphere made Sunday morning more like a party and brought new vitality to what had been a dying congregation.

While there is much that can be done within the church to stimulate joy and celebration, it is really what happens outside the church while God's people are scattered in the world that gives to a church its best party spirit. If the people are having enlivening small-group experiences, winning spiritual victories for justice in the marketplace, and having fruitful times in evangelistic witnessing, then there is much to celebrate when they get together on Sundays. In a real sense, there can be no celebration if there is nothing to celebrate. It is only when people are aware of great things that God is doing in their everyday lives that they have joy to share when they gather together for worship.

SPIRITUAL RENEWAL FROM SMALL GROUPS

The president of Eastern College, Roberta Hestenes, is one of the leaders in promoting small-group renewal for the church. What she has discovered is that when the church initiates a variety of small fellowship groups that meet at various times during the week for study, prayer, and fun, something wonderful happens to the church. By breaking down the congregation of a church into smaller units that better allow for individual expression and spontaneity, all kinds of excitement and good humor can be generated. This inevitably carries over into corporate worship.

I personally belong to a small men's fellowship group that gets together each Tuesday morning for breakfast. We talk about the Bible, our personal lives, what is going on with our families and our jobs, and whatever else may seem important. At these get-togethers, there is always a lot of joking around, as well as serious sharing of personal pains and problems. But there are seldom times that I come out of these encounters devoid of new energy for life and more excitement about God.

In Washington, D.C., there is the somewhat famous Church of the Savior. This church has built its ministry upon what happens in small groups. It has become a model of the great spiritual renewal that can come from the close fellowship experienced in such gatherings. A vital program of social action and evangelism has come out of this church, and there is little question but that the dynamism that drives the program of Church of the Savior is the result of small-group interaction.

Something more than what sociologists can get at emerges when the members of the church in small, face-to-face groups share themselves with each other. There is a spiritual power discovered and released. There is a sense of God's presence and a fulfillment of our Lord's promise that wherever two or three are gathered in His name, He will be in the midst of them (Matt. 18:20).

What happens in these groups is brought into the Sunday services at Church of the Savior, and just about everyone attending worship there feels it. It is the feeling of being at a party.

The Gathered-Scattered Motif

The best pattern for church life is what has often been described as "the gathered-scattered motif." This pattern suggests that the church should gather together for worship and celebration *after* participating with God in winning victories for His Kingdom in the world. If members of the congregation have led people to Christ or have championed the cause of justice, then when they get together they can give testimonies of these things, and in so doing get fellow Christians on to a "high." After experiencing what God has done through them while scattered in the world, Christians find it easy to celebrate when they gather together for worship.

Christians in other countries have become more practiced in this gathered-scattered motif. In New Zealand, hundreds of Christians come together every three years in the city of Wellington to hear lectures on missions, sing songs of worship, and study Scripture. A few years ago, I was the speaker at this missions conference for young adults. Each afternoon, time was set aside for those attending the conference to go out into the city streets and to try to share the gospel with whomever would listen. The plan was for these young Christians to bring with them to the evening worship service any persons that they might have won to Christ during their afternoon of witnessing.

On each of the evenings I was in attendance, there were ample new converts on hand to set the crowd cheering. As each new convert was introduced, there was wild applause and whistling. Every new Christian was hugged and treated like a celebrity.

I have been all over the world, but I have never been to a party that quite equalled those parties in Wellington, New Zealand. What accompanied that un-forgettable conference was partying at its best.

In Australia, I found another example to reinforce this point about the gathered-scattered motif. While on a speaking tour in that "land down under," I was in-vited to speak at a church in the Kings Cross section of the city of Sydney. I was intrigued with what a church was doing in that location, since Kings Cross is infa-mous for being the red-light district of the city. The streets of Kings Cross are lined with night clubs and strip joints, and there is no difficulty spotting prosti-tutes at any hour of the day or night.

What I learned about that church both inspired and challenged me. Its members got together at 8 A.M. for intensive prayer. Then, at 8:30 they scattered throughout the Kings Cross area to share the gospel with whomever they encountered. On that Sunday, as on any normal Sunday, there were prostitutes and drunks left over from the world's kind of partying which had marked the previous Saturday night. The sad, worn-out people, who seemed almost dazed by the degradation of the night before, were loved and cared for by the members of this unusual church. Whenever possible, those picked up on the streets were taken to breakfast, or at least given some coffee. At 11:15 A.M., when the congregation gathered for worship those recruited from the streets were included.

When I finished my sermon there, I gave an invitation to accept Christ as Savior and Lord. Several of the street people who had been brought to the worship service that morning came down the aisle. Their commitments to Christ were greeted by a strong round of applause and shouts of "Praise the Lord!" and "Hallelujah!" Once again, I felt the spirit of a party.

One last example of how what members do in the world can determine the spirit of a congregation on Sunday is in what happened in my own predominantly black church when the Civil Rights Bill finally passed congress. Many of the people of my church had worked long and hard to get support for the bill. Some had marched with Martin Luther King. Some had participated in sit-ins with the Student Non-Violent Coordinating Committee. And almost all of us were members of the NAACP.

A celebration was held on the Sunday following the passage of the bill. The service went on for a couple of hours, and even then could not contain the joy. When our pastor declared "victory," people rose and sang the "Doxology" like I had never heard it before. People were crying tears of joy. It was party time.

While it might not be possible to do things just the way these churches did them, the principle remains the same for every church. If, while being scattered in the world, church members reach out to others in love and experience God accomplishing His work through them, they cannot help but gather together for worship with a sense of joy. Victories in Christ can turn any gathering into a party; but this is especially true for Sunday-morning worship.

Chapter 7

MAKING THE FAMILY
INTO A PARTY

If any sector of Christian living should give evidence of a partying spirit, it is the family. The Christian family in this secular world is one of the last bastions still guided by religious principles prescribed by the church. It is family life that is most clearly delineated by Scripture, with both the apostle Paul and Moses giving careful instructions as to how family relationships are to be lived out before God. If Christianity fails to create celebration for the family, it loses much legitimacy for those who may be considering it for a life commitment.

In spite of these expectations, it is too seldom that families in America reflect the kind of gratifying joy that goes with the Christian party. It is not just those outside the church who are having trouble enjoying life in the family; most Christians, when pressed, will admit that their families, too, lack the kind of fulfillment and fun for which they had hoped.

Unfulfilled Expectations

The increasing failure of the family to provide emotional gratification for its members comes at a time when the pressure to fulfill that role has become particularly pronounced. Talcott Parsons, the former dean of American sociology, explained that providing emotional fulfillment for people has become the primary function of the family. Other institutions have, one by one, stripped it of its former functions. Educating children, giving religious training, supervising health care, and providing training for a life vocation were once the responsibilities of families. Today these things are provided by institutions outside the home. The school and the church are doing what once was the prerogative of parents. The family is no longer an economically productive entity as it was in the farm societies of bygone days.

The family, says Parsons, has become essentially a group of people whose main purpose in being together is to provide mutual emotional gratification and shared joy. In other words, the family is to be a haven in a heartless world. As life becomes stressful and painfully competitive in our advanced technological society, respite and restoration are supposedly to be found in the family. In a world where people live on tiptoe as they play out roles that require them to please people who may not like them, the family is supposedly the setting in which they can relax and be themselves.

In Parsons's view as the world tears us apart, the family is the bonded group that is supposed to put us together again. He expects the family to be an arena for fun. Thus, for Parsons, as for most sociologists, the question might be, "If the family is not a party, then why does it even exist?"

There are many explanations as to why families do not live up to such high expectations. First, there is the diminishing size of the family. Because most people are not farmers who need lots of children to help them make a living, we tend to have fewer and fewer children. We do not need children to care for us in our old age anymore. Social security and pension plans have taken care of that. So we do not have large families in order to ensure that there will be loved ones to care for us in our autumn years.

Add to the diminishing size of American families the propensity toward increased mobility. In this country the average family moves to a new home every five years. These moves uproot most children, disconnecting them from the extended family and curtailing the possibility of long-term friendships. All of this means that the immediate nuclear family, which usually consists of mother, father, and two siblings, is the only stable grouping that most people have as they grow and move from place to place.

This small family unit must bear a heavy emotional load. Its members are supposed to provide for each other all needed encouragement, support, and intimacy.

This tiny conjugal family is supposed to be able to minister to its wounded, patching them up after that mean outside world beats them to pieces.

The task, say such social critics as Christopher Lasch, is just too much for the family to bear. In many instances, the strain this load creates can create a hell for family members. They come to the family bringing so many needs and expecting it to deliver so much that they become resentful when it delivers so little. Most teen-agers, when interviewed by social scientists, indicate disappointment with their parents; and a significant proportion of parents feel cheated with the kinds of kids they have. It seems that most of us expected better.

To make matters worse, most people tend to make their families into dumping grounds. The hostilities that result from oppressive relationships at school and work are often brought home. Such displaced aggression leads family members to say to one another those things they really wish they had had the guts to say to the people who hurt them. The sad fact is that, instead of a haven in a heartless world, many families have become battlefields and psychological wastelands. Against these realities, the necessity for turning our homes into parties becomes an almost Herculean task.

DOING THE RIGHT THING

If the family is to be a party, its members must become committed to doing the right thing. The Bible lays down reciprocal obligations that must be followed as prerequisites to joyful fellowship:

> Submitting yourselves one to another in the fear of God. Wives, submit yourselves unto your own husbands, as unto the Lord. . . . Husbands, love your wives, even as Christ also loved the church, and gave himself for it. . . .
> Children, obey your parents in the Lord: for this is right. Honour thy father and mother; which is the first commandment with promise. . . . And ye fathers, provoke not your children to wrath: but bring them up in the nurture and admonition of the Lord. (Eph. 5:21–22, 25; 6:1–2, 4)

This may appear a bit incongruous to partying. Partying, in the modern world, seems to mean just the opposite of fulfilling obligations. Usually partying denotes letting yourself go and doing your own thing. Of course, that is exactly what is wrong with the world's parties and why they so often are disastrous.

The famous University of California sociologist Robert Bellah, in his best-selling book *Habits of the Heart*, argues convincingly that Americans have lost a sense of duty in personal relationships. Victimized by some "pop" psychologists, they have made the quest for individual fulfillment their ultimate goal. In seeking "self-actualization" and "the realization of their human potentialities," Americans often set aside obligations to spouses, parents, and children. They read too many books (like *Jonathan Livingston Seagull*) that nurture the belief that it is all right to shrug off the expectations which go with our relationships with others in favor of the pursuit of our own personal happiness.

How many of us have seen, on TV shows like "Geraldo" or "Donahue," some guest who explains how necessary it was to break away from the restraints of marriage and family in order to "become"? The joyful life seems increasingly defined as "doing your own thing" even if some people unfortunately get hurt in the process.

CREATING FAMILY PARTIES

Over and against this libertine pattern that goes with the world's kind of "fulfilled living" stands a biblical model that calls us to responsibility to one another—especially within the family. It is within the context of obligation that God's kind of party takes place.

The first obligation is to put the joy of the family above the demands of other people and associations. Business, sports, and outside friends should all be put second to the family. The family should eat together if at all possible. And the meals should not be rush jobs where people eat and immediately run off to other activities. The meal, as in Bible times, should be treated as a sacred time. It should be a time of sharing and learning from each other. It should be an unhurried time of being together. A lot of effort is required to accomplish these ends in our helter-skelter world, but the results make the effort a worthwhile investment.

On the speaking circuit, I have gotten to know Leo Buscaglia, the famous author and television personality. Leo told me of his own family life and of the partying nature of dinner hour at his home. He came from a very large family and, in accord with Italian custom, eating together was a very special time. At every meal, each person was supposed to share with the rest of the family something that had been learned that day. Then his father would lead a discussion on each bit of information that was shared. Every family member was made to feel that his or her contribution was important; in the process, his or her sense of self-worth was enhanced.

In my own family, each of us had an obligation to share something "funny" that had happened during the day. It was no wonder that all of the Campolos became incurable storytellers. When our family got together at meal time, we all knew we were in for a good time. Meal time was party time at our house.

Nothing should be allowed to interfere with these family get-togethers, not even church. Too often, church activities become family threatening. The church that pulls the father away for one activity one night, disengages the kids from the family another night, and then has special programs for mothers still another night can do a great deal of harm to the family fabric. The church ought to enhance, not prevent, the family party. And family members should not feel guilty about making the family party a primary activity in their lives. (And don't forget to take the phone off the hook.)

Secondly, the family must recognize its obligation to celebrate special days. Christmas and Thanksgiving must be planned to be extra special. I once made fun of my mother and sisters when they planned a time for caroling and a time when each of us was expected to entertain the rest of the family. I acted disgusted with the demands that my mother placed on each of us to "perform" for the extended family every time we got together.

But that was before I understood what she was doing for us. Birthdays were celebrations, as were graduations, christenings, and wedding engagements. Whenever the Campolo relatives got together, each child was expected to perform. We were a poor family, but my parents made sure that each of my sisters and I took music lessons. While only my sister Rose became an accomplished musician, each of us became good enough to put on a show when the family got together for celebrations. For our family, every holiday was an excuse for a party, and every party turned into a show time.

Sometimes my wife reminds me that it was easy for the Campolos to "carry on" like we did on holidays. "After all," she says, "the Campolos are all extroverts."

But I have to ask if we are extroverts because of genetics or if we are the way we are because of how we were raised. There is no doubt that we Campolos were raised to be a partying people who enjoyed being on stage, and that entertaining one another became, for each of us, our greatest joy. Whatever criticisms might be leveled at the "showoff" tendencies that our upbringing may have nurtured in us, there is no doubt that each of us grew up feeling important. How could it have been otherwise, when we were made the recipients of standing ovations ever since we could remember?

SHARING HISTORY

There is still another thing that can be done to make the family into a party. That is to turn your family experiences into "a story." Robert Bellah contends that people become a joyful community with a sense of belonging when they share what he calls a "common narrative." In other words, a family is a party when its members come together and share an array of stories, particularly funny stories, of things that they once did together. Some of the best fun times a family can have occur when everybody sits around the table after a good meal and tells old yarns and tales of bygone days.

As a boy, I remember those drawn-out Sunday evenings when we would entertain each other by remembering for the hundredth time episodes of our family's past. No other party could be as good. No other celebration could be more exuberant. No other festival could be more zany. The same goes for my present family, made up of my wife and two children. My son and daughter are grown now and out of the house. Still, when we have a family get-together and finish off a good dinner with a couple of hours of storytelling the gathering becomes the best kind of party.

Sometimes the stories become embroidered to enhance their quality and drama. Sometimes dialogue that could not have been possibly overheard is reported. Sometimes, as my son tells me, "we remember big." But it does not seem to matter. It's party time.

It is fun to tell about such things as the time my wife Peggy bought a stereo for my car and secretly had it installed. She put in a tape with a John Philip Sousa march on it, turned up the volume full blast, and left the car parked for me to pick up at the airport. I got in at two in the morning on my way home from a speaking engagement, unaware that I had been set up. I got into my car, turned on the ignition, and was greeted by a thousand-decibel rendition of "Stars and Stripes Forever."

Then there was the time my ten-year-old son enthralled a crowd of tourists in Chartres, France, by providing a lecture on the history and architecture of the cathedral. Just before our trip to Europe, he had been in a special art class at school that had spent several weeks studying the cathedral. When we visited the place, Bart started to tell us what he had learned, pointing out and explaining the various features of this architectural masterpiece. His strong voice soon attracted a crowd and in no time he was transformed into an unofficial tour guide.

We love to remember the time when our daughter Lisa was in the second grade, and Peggy and I forgot to go to a play in which she had a leading role. We had had automobile trouble that day and in the upset had forgotten about Lisa's big debut as an actress. The play was about prehistoric dinosaurs and she had had the part of a triceratops.

At four in the afternoon Lisa's little figure stood in the doorway of the kitchen, still dressed in her triceratops costume. "You didn't come!" she sadly accused us. "I looked and looked, and you didn't come!" She just kept saying it over and over again. And there was no consoling her with explanations.

What makes this sad event funny is that ever since then we have tried to make it up to her by buying her triceratops paraphernalia. We have bought her lunch boxes and pens with triceratops pictures on them. We have bought her stuffed triceratopses and inflatable triceratopses. It has become a real joke with us now that she is grown up and a lawyer. We still buy her triceratops "things" for birthdays and Christmas.

The story of her part in that little play has become part of our family's shared narrative. Telling that story is part of what we do when we all get together. It is in telling stories like this that we are able to transform a "get-together" into a party.

Stop to think about it! Doesn't every good party involve stories that entertain? Isn't every good time a time of remembering good tales of the past?

It is very important for families to keep the stories of their past alive. Telling and retelling the cute and funny things that have happened makes for a sense of belonging, and creates a sense of shared history. It is part of what makes people feel their importance in the family fun. It can be said that such storytelling is so much a part of what it means to be a family that there *is* no family without a shared narrative. The family that tells stories together stays together. A party with stories is what family is all about.

Chapter 8

MAKING A PARTY

OUT OF WORK

Eastern College, where I teach, is located just west of Philadelphia and less than fifty miles from what is called "the Pennsylvania Dutch country." This Pennsylvania Dutch country is home to a large Mennonite community. I often take my sociology students to visit these Anabaptist Christians because their understanding of the Sermon on the Mount and the Book of Acts has led them to try a variety of unique experiments in Christian living.

One of the most interesting and inspiring things we observe on these trips is a special activity that the Mennonites have developed for older women. They do quilting. Each morning, a bus goes around Lancaster County and picks up about a dozen women, most of whom are widows, and brings them to a warehouse in the town of Akron. These women then spend the day together making quilts. They sit on the four sides of a frame and work on quilts which, when completed, sell for hundreds of dollars.

As they do their quilting, they talk and joke. They make their work time visiting time. It's a joy just to watch them having such a good time with each other. They make work into a party. This is an almost ideal way to work.

In the small town of Rifton, just north of New York City, there is another Anabaptist community that is home to the Hutterites. My son and I recently visited this community of more than three hundred Christians who live together in what they call the Bruderhoff.

The means by which this Christian commune supports itself is a factory that produces equipment needed to make life easier for people with physical disabilities. These Hutterites produce special wheelchairs, walking helps, bathtub accessories, and toys which are in great demand all around the world.

They sell these things at very reasonable prices. It is obvious that the prices could be at least 100 percent higher than they are, but, as one of the leaders of the Bruderhoff explained to me, "We could make a great deal more money from what we produce. But we make more than enough to meet our needs, and by setting low prices we make the equipment affordable to many who otherwise could not buy these things."

When I visited the factory, both my son and I were duly impressed. We saw men and women as well as boys and girls working together in what was obviously an enjoyable setting. Parents were having a great time showing their sons and daughters how to use the tools and run the machinery. There was obvious pride in workmanship and a joyful sharing of chores. Once again, I saw people who had turned their workplace into the setting for a party.

PRODUCE WHAT IS GOOD

E. F. Schumacher and other Christian economists have written extensively on what is required to transform work from oppressive labor into joyful celebration. A primary factor is making sure what is produced through the work is worthwhile. So many products are unnecessary or even evil. For instance, it seems unlikely to me that much spiritual gratification could be gained from producing cigarettes. Knowing that cancer and death can come to those who use what is produced has got to take away the sense of having done good after a day's work. And I often wonder how the production of bombs affects those who work in munitions factories, or how those who make styrofoam cups react when they learn that what they produce can contribute to an ecological disaster capable of causing pain for their children and grandchildren. What people produce must be good for their fellow human beings if the producers are to be able to celebrate their work and offer it up as thanks to God.

And whatsoever ye do in word or deed, do all in the
name of the Lord Jesus, giving thanks to God and
the Father by him. (Col. 3:17)

Next, work should utilize the creative gifts of the
workers. When a job is monotonous or involves repeti-
tion that allows for no ingenuity or imaginative skill,
most workers die a slow psychological death in their
daily labor. Unfortunately, a good proportion of the
work force performs this kind of work.

When I was in college, I had a summer job that involved working on an assembly line. I ran a machine.
All that was required of me was to watch the thing
punch out metal washers. If the machine got jammed,
I pulled a "release" lever and cleared out the metal
pieces that had caused the trouble. The machine seldom jammed more than a couple of times a day.

The boredom of the job was almost more than I could
bear. The only way I survived that summer was to be
absent when I was present. In other words, it was only
by transporting myself via my imagination into happier
places and more interesting activities that I was able to
make it through a working day. The main thing that
kept me sane that summer was the knowledge that the
job would only be for a matter of weeks. I cannot even
imagine how I would have handled it if I had thought
that was to be my job for the rest of my life.

I do not want to give the impression that it is only on
the assembly line that people experience a deprivation

of job satisfaction. According to Paul Goodman, the author of *Growing Up Absurd,* more than 70 percent of all American workers get little or no gratification out of their jobs, and only 10 percent of these people work on assembly lines. In the words of a famous man, "most men live out their lives in quiet desperation."

Lastly, if work is to be a party, it should be carried out in the context of sociability. In the Oneida Colony, one of the Utopian experiments of the nineteenth century, work was especially designed to be carried out in the context of a partying fellowship. From those who lived in the Oneida Colony comes this report:

> As children, we loved to visit the various departments they used to have: the laundry, the kitchen, the fruit cellar, the bakery, the dairy, the dining room, the ice house, the tailor shop—they even had a Turkish bath in the basement. The thing is that small groups of people worked side by side in most of these places, and they were able to talk with each other as they worked.
>
> It's hard to explain, but my mother used to tell me that no matter how menial the job was, they were so busy talking to each other that the time always flew. It was this sort of thing, year after year, that gave rise to a kindred spirit. (Kephart, W. J., *The Family, Society, and the Individual,* 6th ed., Harper & Row, 1988, p. 103)

I think when labor unions press employers to make things better for workers, they should put the opportunity for enjoyable interaction on the job at the top of their list of demands. It seems to me that having the possibility for fellowship with other workers is more important than a raise in salary or the addition of "perks."

THE "KNIGHT OF FAITH"

Unfortunately, a lot of people do not have much choice about what they produce, where they work, or what they actually do on the job. There are many who lack viable options when it comes to making a living and who are stuck in dehumanizing work situations. They would like to quit, but their obligations to support families keeps them in their drudgery.

Those who sense that they are trapped in such situations should not throw up their hands in dismay or give up on the possibility of partying. There is a spirit of partying which individuals can carry, even into the most difficult of work settings. There is a quality of the soul that enables Christians to possess a joy which they can share with fellow workers in even the most bleak circumstances.

In the factory where I had my summer assembly-line job there was such a person. I talked with him before and after work. I enjoyed lingering with him on the parking lot and I would always seek him out at lunch and during breaks. He was just fun to be around. Jesus was like that. He was the life of the party and wherever He went, He brought "the party" with Him. It is no wonder that He attracted followers or that even the most unlikely sorts became His disciples.

Søren Kierkegaard, the brilliant Danish existentialist philosopher, understood well the notion that the joyfulness and celebration that go with a good party are usually traits inherent in the partygoers own personality. Partying, as Kierkegaard points out, can be an attitude toward life that one carries into the work place and which transforms that setting into something that tastes of the Kingdom of God.

In describing what an ideal Christian is like, he presents a person whom he calls, "The Knight of Faith." This man, says Kierkegaard, looks like a "tax collector." There is nothing special about him. As he comes home from work, he thinks of the cherry pie his wife has baked for him and how much he will enjoy it. With deep appreciation he breathes the air. He experiences everything that an ordinary person might experience, but he does so in an extraordinary way. The Knight of Faith is resigned to whatever life might bring. With childlike anticipation, he smiles benevolently at the world and accepts its wonder. He lives with a sense of gratitude and this makes him a man to be envied.

This disposition toward work has a contemporary expression in the former president of Haverford College. Haverford, as you may know, is always ranked in the top five colleges of the country. It is a school that has high prestige because of outstanding scholarship.

The president of Haverford had all the credentials that go with being part of a sophisticated aristocracy. But each summer during his tenure as president, John Coleman would take off from his academic responsibilities, go to a community where he was virtually unknown, and take a job as a garbage collector.

This college president claimed that being a garbage collector gave him a necessary perspective on life and also provided him with a chance to judge academia through the eyes of a manual laborer. This erudite scholar learned a lot about life by spending his summers incognito working as a garbage collector. But he also brought something to the job. He had an array of stories to tell his co-workers that they had never heard before. He had a fun-loving attitude which he introduced to them. He taught them to sing on the job, and most importantly, he taught them clever ways of putting down those uppity people who treat garbage collectors like trash.

After all, he knew all about such upper-crust people from personal experience. By helping the men he worked with to see the ludicrous nature of those who disdained them, he helped to get them to laugh at people who, up until then, had left them hurt and sad. The college-president-become-garbage-collector taught his new friends how to make their workday into a party.

All of this adds up to the simple declaration that each person should learn to bloom where he or she is planted. You cannot always control where you will be set down in this life. But you certainly can control what happens there. You have it within your power to turn the place where you work into a party, providing you, yourself, have become a party person.

What you become on the individual level has a great deal to do with what happens at the place where you work each day. That is why the next section of this little book must deal with how to become a party person and explain how being such a person is at the core of what it means to be a Christian.

Chapter 9

GETTING INTO
THE PARTY SPIRIT

"The party" is not simply an event. It is an attitude. It is a disposition that should be carried by Christians wherever they go. Christians should be people who create celebrations wherever they are placed. Members of the New Testament church were certainly capable of doing this. Even when imprisoned, those first-century Christians were able to create a party atmosphere, to the bafflement of their wardens and fellow prisoners. Consider the imprisonment of Paul and Silas:

> And when they had laid many stripes upon them, they cast them into prison, charging the jailer to keep them safely: Who, having received such a charge, thrust them into the inner prison, and made their feet fast in the stocks. And at midnight Paul and Silas prayed, and sang praises unto God: and the prisoners heard them. (Acts 16:23–25)

Undoubtedly, this celebrative lifestyle was part of what made early Christianity so infectious. Both pagans and Jews must have found something very attractive about a religious faith that enabled people to sing and praise, no matter what the circumstances.

PARTYING OUR WAY TO THE ABUNDANT LIFE

Whatever Christianity may have gained or lost since that first generation of believers, the loss of that joyful spontaneity which Scripture compares to the giddy excitement of the first love of a teen-ager (See Revelation 2:4.) can be ill afforded. It is this that contributes so much toward providing what Jesus called "the abundant life."

More directly, let me assert that becoming a Christian is becoming a very special kind of a "party animal." As I argued earlier, the kind of party that is played out in the Christian community is far different from that which is indulged in by those who do not walk in the ways of the world. So the kind of "party animal" the Christian becomes is far different from that which is being created in the libertine society in which most of us must live out our lives.

Whatever else Christian conversion involves, let it be very clear that coming into the "born again" experience is coming into a state of joyful celebration. A Christian is not simply a person who accepts some biblically proven propositional truths about who Jesus was and what He accomplished in His death and resurrection; it also involves a subjective decision to surrender to Jesus and to allow Him to invade one's personality. Becoming a Christian means being permeated by the presence of Jesus. It is to allow this Person who is alive in the world and is as close as the air that one breathes to be inhaled and enjoyed.

Something happens when one realizes that Jesus is not just an objective fact of history but also a personal presence blazingly alive in "the ground of one's being." That realization, according to the famous founder of the psychology of religion, William James, may come suddenly or gradually. But when that awareness that Jesus is an indwelling presence becomes full blown there is always a sense of ecstasy. Not everyone can describe this experience with the eloquence of the seventeenth-century existentialist philosopher/scientist, Blaise Pascal, but all who have come to know this indwelling presence can identify with his description:

> From about half past ten
> in the evening to about half
> an hour after midnight
>   Fire.
>
> God of Abraham, God of Isaac
> God of Jacob, Not the God of
> philosophers and scholars. Absolute
> certainty; Beyond Reason!

> Joy, Peace.
> Forgetfulness of the world and
> everything but God.
>
> The world has not known thee,
> But I have known thee.
> Joy! Joy! Joy! Tears
> of Joy.

When the apostle Paul speaks of what happens to the person who surrenders to Jesus, he talks of becoming a new person (2 Cor. 5:17), of being possessed of an explosive inner dynamic (Rom. 1:16), and of coming alive:

> And if Christ be in you, the body is dead because of sin; but the Spirit is life because of righteousness. But if the Spirit of him that raised up Jesus from the dead dwell in you, he that raised up Christ from the dead shall also quicken your mortal bodies by his Spirit that dwelleth in you. (Rom. 8:10–11)

"Do It Again!"

There is a celebrative mood as one goes through the process of leaving behind the former self which was permeated by a demonic spirit, and drinking in the joy of the resurrected Jesus, whom Christians call the Holy Spirit.

With God there is a childlike giddiness, and all who surrender to Him become like little children. Lord Chesterton once argued that when it comes to this kind of joy, God may be the only thoroughly childlike spirit left in the universe, while all the rest of us have lost this ecstasy because of sin.

Chesterton asks us to consider how God might have created daisies. Did He create them all at once, with one swoop of His hand? Or did God create them one by one, experiencing childlike delight in each new flower?

If you throw a child up in the air and bounce the child off your knee there is every chance that the child will shout out, "Do it again!" And if you do it again, you probably will get the same response. In all likelihood, each time you toss the child in the air the laughter will become more uncontrolled. Twenty times later the child, never tiring of the fun, can be counted on to be overwhelmed with hysteria while still shouting, "Do it again!"

So it might be with God, suggests Chesterton. In the beginning God may have created one daisy, and something within His spontaneous, childlike spirit whispered, *Do it again!* And daisy number two came into being. And once again God said, "Do it again!" And there was a third, and then a fourth, and then a fifth daisy. And so He went on creating daisies. Until after a hundred billion trillion daisies the great creator God, who spun the galaxies into space and created all the animals, that same God is still creating daisies, and shouting with childlike glee, "Do it again!"

To be "saved" is to be in His image and in His likeness. To be Christian is to transcend the sense of dullness and boredom that seems so evident in our world and to be able to greet even that which is repetitious in our mundane world with joyous declarations of "Do it again!"

This energizing joy that comes from God as one of the fruits of His Spirit (Gal. 5:22–23) makes us into people who cannot help but share our laughter and fun. It is out of this God-created effervescence that I find that I must be at play even when that play disrupts the boring sullenness of some social situations.

For instance, one day I got on an elevator in the World Trade Center in New York City. It was one of those express elevators that goes fifty floors without making a stop. The elevator was filled with briefcase-bearing, somber businessmen on their way to "heavy" meetings.

As I got on the elevator, a feeling of fun ran through me. And, instead of turning and facing the door, as we are all socialized to do, I just stood there facing the people. When the elevator doors closed, I smiled coyly and announced "We're going to be traveling together for quite a while, you know." And then I added, "What do you say we all sing?"

The reaction was wonderful! They did! You should have been there as a dozen or so businessmen threw

aside their put-on seriousness and joined me in a ring-
ing rendition of "You Are My Sunshine." By the time
the elevator got to the fiftieth floor we were all laugh-
ing. Being a Christian on that elevator was turning
some men, made numb by the affairs of this world, into
"party animals."

EVANGELIZING THROUGH PARTIES

Party-spreading can, on occasion, be overtly evangelistic. By that I mean that creating a party can also create the context for winning people to Christ. One such
case in point occurred two years ago when I was in
Rome, Georgia, to do some preaching at a small Baptist
college. My hosts housed me at the local Holiday Inn
where there was a friendly bar that featured some good
country-western music. Following my first evening
message, I returned to the Holiday Inn along with a
young man who had come along to share in my ministry and find out something of what being an evange-
list is like. The two of us passed the bar and were easily
seduced by a couple of musicians who were in there
belting out "I'm Sending You a Big Bouquet of Roses."

I asked my partner, "How about going in and listen-
ing for a while?"

At first he was a bit reluctant since we were then
cast in the role of traveling evangelists. But when I
assured him it would be O.K. if we did not order
booze, he agreed.

There were about fifteen or twenty people in the bar and it seemed as though nobody was really paying any attention to the couple up front who were strumming their guitars and singing their lungs out. My friend and I took a table right up front where we really could get into the music and cheer on this man and woman who were trying so hard. We tapped the table in rhythm to the beat of each song and showed our appreciation by clapping and cheering wildly after each number. Soon we had the other people in the place wide awake; after a few more songs they were right with us as we cheered on the singers.

The appreciative performers asked us if we had any favorites and I, in turn, asked them if they knew any gospel music. They did. And before anybody realized what was happening they were letting go with the likes of "This Little Light of Mine" and "I'll Fly Away." The crowd loved it and soon everyone was singing along with them. We had turned that bar into an old-fashioned hymn-sing. A good time was had by all.

When the set was over and the singing couple took a break they came over to our table and sat down to visit. We talked for a few minutes and soon we got around to who we were and why we were in town. This dear man and woman told us about themselves and how they loved playing music even though they had a hard time making any money at it.

In the course of our little time together they explained how they had gone to church a long time ago.

They told us that they believed in God, but had gotten away from religion. I ended up asking them if they wanted to pray with me and to rededicate themselves to the Lord. So there, in that bar, I prayed with them that they might grow in faith and dependence on Christ.

The next morning I was scheduled to speak at the college chapel. When I got into the pulpit and looked over the congregation, I was really pleased to see my two singing friends from the bar sitting in the front row. At the end of my sermon I gave an invitation for those who wanted to give their lives to Christ to come down the aisle and kneel at the altar. These country-western singers were the first ones to come forward.

I have kept in touch with these two music-loving Christians over the years. They still play in bars. But wherever they play, they do some gospel music and give their testimonies as to how they got to know Jesus in a Holiday Inn in Rome, Georgia. I don't know, but I kind of think God loves what they do.

Isn't it amazing what can come out of a party?

WELCOME-HOME PARTIES

Whenever anybody becomes a Christian, we ought to have a party. Certainly Jesus felt this way. Our Lord told us the story of the prodigal son just to make this point. After the wayward boy in this story returns home, the Bible says:

But the father said to his servants, Bring forth the best robe, and put it on him; and put a ring on his hand, and shoes on his feet: And bring hither the fatted calf, and kill it; and let us eat, and be merry: For this my son was dead, and is alive again; he was lost and is found. And they began to be merry. (Luke 15:22–24)

It seems only right that individuals coming into the fellowship of believers should be welcomed by celebration. The Bible clearly makes it clear that whenever a person repents and surrenders to God, the angels in heaven send up a hoorah and have a party (Luke 15:7). Therefore, it only seems fitting that we should replicate on earth the celebrations that take place in heaven whenever somebody "comes home to God."

I was talking to a missionary friend who worked among Muslim people in Pakistan. He explained to me that the first time he baptized a convert from Islam to Christianity the young man bolted out of the water and yelled "Hallelujah!" Then he ran to his friends who had witnessed the baptism, joined hands with them, and wildly danced for joy. Onlookers were sure that such partying antics are always a part of Christian baptism. So now what that first new Christian in the town did that day has become a practice followed by every new Christian who is baptized. After all, the people in that little town in Pakistan are only following the example of the angels and partying over the homecoming of one of God's children.

Chapter 10

SUFFERING THROUGH
THE PARTY

A misconception easily promoted by talking about the Kingdom of God as a party is that Christians should be smiling and happy all the time. There are some who suggest that those who have been "saved" have no right to be sorrowful. Such people can make us feel guilty if we show any signs of being downhearted.

Let it be herewith declared: Christians cry. They are followers of One who was Himself a Man of sorrows and acquainted with grief. Christians go through the valley of the shadow of death. They are followers of One who trembled and sweat blood in a place called Gethsemane. Christians know that the shortest verse in the Bible simply says, "Jesus wept" (John 11:35).

A young man who had turned his back on the church told me that he had no time for Christians because, as far as he was concerned, they were all a bunch of phonies. I assumed he meant that, as he viewed them, Christians did not live consistent lives—that their everyday behavior did not measure up to their declared beliefs nor their convictions about how Christians should live. In short, their walk did not go with their talk.

He admitted there was some of that in his cynicism, but the basis for his judgment went far deeper. Years earlier he had had a little sister who had been stricken with cancer. He spent months watching her little body wither up while she suffered excruciating pain. In the midst of this ordeal he asked the usual question of "why?" and, like all others who have ever asked it, came up blank.

He found that he could live with the silence of God. What he could not live with were the pretenses of Christians in the face of this tragedy. Those in his church, and especially those in his immediate family, said they had no sorrow because they knew his little sister had gone to be with Jesus. They smiled those plastic smiles that are often put on by Christians on such occasions, and they told each other they knew only joy in spite of what had happened.

The night following the funeral, this young man went into his church to think and pray. He sat in the balcony of the darkened church. Then, after he had been there for several hours, his father, who was the pastor of the church, came in. Unaware that his son was watching him from the balcony, he slowly walked to the altar and began to cry. The crying turned into wailing and uncontrolled sobbing. Silently, the young man watched his father pour out his soul in sorrow. Then, suddenly, his father stopped the crying, looked up at the painting of Christ that was placed above the altar, shook his fist at it and screamed, 'DAMN YOU!'

When the boy returned home later that night, he found his father once again wearing that forced, artificial smile, and pretending that, as a Christian, he had no agony or disappointment with God. That did it for this young man. He wanted no part of a religion that led people to pretend they had no heartbreak when they really did. He wanted nothing to do with a church that made him feel guilty for his heavy heart.

CRYING—BUT NOT COLLAPSING

Christians are allowed to cry. Indeed, the sensitivities they develop in their close relationship with Christ make them very prone to tears. What is different about Christians is that their sorrow does not lead to despair. They do not wring their hands as do those who have no hope. In the midst of their sorrow they are able to reassure each other that a better day is coming. They are able to encourage one another that the sting of tragedy will one day be swallowed up in a great victory party.

O death, where is thy sting? O grave, where is thy victory? The sting of death is sin; and the strength of sin is the law. But thanks be to God, which giveth us the victory through our Lord Jesus Christ. (1 Cor. 15:55–57)

We Christians must be reminded from time to time that God's party is still coming. We can have foretastes of it. But we cannot enter into the fullness of the party until that day when our Lord and Saviour returns to abolish sickness, sin, and death, and institute that party which will last forever. In the meantime, there is a lot to cry about, and from time to time, we will be led to cry; but our sorrow is qualitatively different from that of those who are without Christ.

This reality has seldom been made more clear to me than it was when I participated in a forum on death and dying at the College of Physicians in Philadelphia. One of the speakers was a supervisor for a home for the Jewish elderly. Those whom he served were strict Orthodox Jews, as he was himself. As such, neither they nor he had any clear theological convictions about the afterlife. They believed that this life is all there is, and that death is annihilation. This man went on to explain how difficult it was for those at his home whenever anyone died. Those who remained had little hope of ever seeing the deceased person again. The finality of death in the minds of these Orthodox Jews always left them in despair.

Contrast this with the beliefs and feelings of the people in my home church, Mount Carmel Baptist Church in West Philadelphia, which, as I said earlier, happens to be a predominantly black church. I attended my first funeral at Mount Carmel when I was twenty years old. Clarence, a college friend of mine, had been killed in a subway-train accident and his friends were all overcome with grief.

For the first fifteen minutes of the service, the pastor brilliantly expounded upon what the Bible says about the promise of the resurrection and the joys of being with Christ. Then he came down from the platform and went over to the right side of the sanctuary, where the family of my dead friend was seated in the first three rows. There, he spoke special words of comfort for them.

Then the pastor did a most unusual thing. He went over to the open casket and spoke as though to the corpse. I can still hear him saying, "Clarence! Clarence! There were a lot of things we should have said to you when you were alive that we never got around to saying to you. And I want to say them now."

What followed was a beautiful litany of memories of things that Clarence had done for many of us and for the church. The list recalled how lovingly my friend had served others without thought of reward. When he had finished, my pastor looked at Clarence's body and said, "Well, Clarence, that's it. I've got nothing else to say except this: Good night, Clarence. Good Night!" And with that he slammed down the lid of the casket as a stunned silence fell over the congregation.

Then a beautiful smile slowly lit up the pastor's face and he shouted, "and I know that God is going to give Clarence a good morning!"

With that the choir rose to its feet and started singing "On that great gettin' up morning we shall rise, we shall rise!" All of us in the congregation rose to our feet and started singing it with them. There was clapping and crying. But they were tears of laughter. Everywhere I looked, there were smiles amidst the tears. Celebration had broken out in the face of death. Something of the party that is to come had broken into that church. A foretaste of the joy that will one day be shared by us all was temporarily ours, a glimpse of the party prepared for all of those who die in Christ was had, and death had been swallowed up in victory.

After that, we would think of Clarence from time to time. And we would miss him. We would cry for Clarence now and then. But our tears would not be like those who have no hope. We Christians can cope with tragedy and sorrow because we know that in the midst of everything that is happening—good or bad, painful or happy, ugly or beautiful—God is at work. And out of it all He will make a party for all who are willing to attend.

FOUNDED UPON A ROCK

Recently, a woman asked me what scripture I used when I tried to help people who were going through difficult and sorrowful times. I told her that I usually used Matthew 7:24–27:

> [Jesus said,] Therefore whosoever heareth these sayings of mine, and doeth them, I will liken him unto a wise man, which built his house upon a rock: And the rain descended, and the floods came, and the winds blew, and beat upon that house; and it fell not: for it was founded upon a rock. And every one that heareth these sayings of mine, and doeth them not, shall be likened unto a foolish man, which built his house upon the sand: And the rain descended, and the floods came, and the winds blew, and beat upon that house; and it fell: and great was the fall of it.

What these verses make clear is that the storms of life hit all kinds of people. The rains fall on the just and on the unjust (Matt. 5:45). The same kinds of hardships hit those who walk with Jesus as hit those who do not. The prosperity theology that suggests that bad things do not happen to good people is a lie. Day in and day out, we meet Christians who suffer.

What is different about the Christians is that they are grounded on the rock—which is the promise of God. Christians find in Christ a firm foundation that enables them to survive the storms. When they are battered by life's circumstances, Christians do not collapse. Like the house built upon the rock, they endure.

When I explained all of this to the woman, she responded, "Is that all? Is that the best you can do? Is the strength to endure all that you have to offer?"

"Don't take what I said lightly," I answered. "The strength to endure is much more important than you think. But that is not all," I went on to say. "The promise of God is that one day He will gather us all together in a place where tears are wiped away and where we will have a party which He Himself will personally host."

It is that future breaking into the midst of our present sufferings that enables us to conquer our sorrows (Rom. 8:37). Christians cry; but on the other side of their sadness they know there is a party.

CELEBRATING THE FUTURE OF THE WORLD

There are a lot of people who look at human history and find nothing to party about. They pick up the newspapers and see little that can be regarded as "good news." They read about violent revolutions in Latin America, an AIDS epidemic that threatens to kill one out of every four persons in America, rising crime rates, the demise of the family, and the increase in international terrorism.

In the face of these realities, people are apt to shake their heads and claim there is nothing to party about these days. They see things as bad and getting worse.

Doomsayers at one time in America seemed limited to those who preached the fundamentalist gospel.

Leaning on their Scofield Bibles, these preachers of the Word predicted an increasing tendency toward sin and decadence until that day when the world would be so bad that Jesus would have to return to put a stop to it all. There seemed to be a degree of satisfaction in any news that things in this world were falling apart. As they understood it, the faster this world went down the tubes, the more the Lord's return would be hastened.

But nowadays it is not just the dispensationalist preachers who have dire predictions about the future of the human race. Environmentalists have joined the chorus of doomsayers, and with good reason. If we keep on pumping chlorofluorocarbons into the atmosphere every time we use spray cans for paint or deodorants, it won't be long before we destroy the layer of ozone that protects us from those sun rays which would give us all skin cancer. Unless we stop dumping garbage and sewage into the ocean, we soon will destroy the plankton that provide the oxygen that we breathe. And if we do not end the rapid destruction of the Amazon jungle, the world will soon experience climate changes that will not only bring droughts and desertification in South America (which may already be the case) but will turn the entire planet into a meteorological disaster.

There is much evidence to support a negative prognosis for what Hal Lindsay would call "The Late Great Planet Earth." In light of this evidence that demands a verdict of hopelessness, many will ask how it is possible to have anything to party about. My response to the doomsayers is that they are only partly right.

While it is true that terrible things are happening, it is also true that many wonderful things are taking place. The problem with most observers is that they tend to see either one side or the other. They either see the kingdom of evil taking over human history and ignore the growth and victories of the Kingdom of God. Or they become enamored by any evidence of progress and take any signs of peacemaking as proof that utopia is just around the corner.

In the early part of this century, those preachers and theologians who promoted what has come to be called the Social Gospel often got carried away with their optimism and predicted that we were just a decade or two away from bringing in the Kingdom of God all on our own. These liberals were sure that evil could be defeated by spiritually inspired "liberal" Christians who would remake the world in accord with what God had always wanted.

Of course, such optimism about the future was contagious during the first couple of decades of the 1900s. Everything seemed to be getting better and better back then.

But that unbridled optimism about the future was not to last. Human limitations were soon to become all too obvious. The unsinkable ship *Titanic* sank! The war that was to end all wars didn't! The eugenically created superman turned out to be a monster! The dream of inevitable progress fell apart.

Fundamentalists were never deceived by all of those positive press clippings that heralded the emergence of a more perfect world. They knew their Bibles too well to believe that unregenerate humanity was capable of such achievements. Their scripturally grounded doctrine of original sin made them cynical about the promises of a better world. To them, the world was doomed and the best thing the church could do was to save as many souls as possible from out of this world before the whole thing went under.

A SENSE OF GOD AT WORK

The Social Gospelers and the fundamentalists each had part of the truth. Indeed, evil is abounding wherever we turn. But the Kingdom of God is also growing up right in front of our eyes. Those who have eyes ought to see it.

What is really taking place is that both the kingdom of evil and the Kingdom of God are growing simultaneously. Evil has never been more evident; but at the same time the church is having its best days. The fires of revival are everywhere. In Africa, south of the Sahara, more than 50 percent of the population is in Christian worship on any given Sunday. In Korea, the pace of church growth is so rapid as to be difficult to imagine. And in Latin America, evangelism is reaping an unparalleled harvest.

There is a sense of God at work in the political and economic sectors of this world as well. The rapid disintegration of the Iron Curtain is an answer to prayer. The movement toward the end of apartheid in South Africa is a sign of the working of the Lord. An emerging peace plan from the president of Costa Rica offers new hope for Central America.

This observation that the kingdom of evil and the Kingdom of God are growing up simultaneously is amply alluded to in the parable of the wheat and the tares as told by Jesus:

> Another parable put he forth unto them, saying, The kingdom of heaven is likened unto a man which sowed good seed in his field: But while men slept, his enemy came and sowed tares among the wheat, and went his way. But when the blade was sprung up, and brought forth fruit, then appeared the tares also.
>
> So the servants of the householder came and said unto him, Sir, didst not thou sow good seed in thy field? from whence then hath it tares? He said unto them, An enemy hath done this. The servants said unto him, Wilt thou then that we go and gather them up?
>
> But he said, Nay; lest while ye gather up the tares, ye root up also the wheat with them. Let both grow together until the harvest: and in the time of harvest I will say to the reapers, Gather ye together first the

tares, and bind them in bundles to burn them: but gather the wheat into my barn. (Matt. 13:24–30)

In light of what the Bible tells us about where history is going, it is easy to see why we have much to party about, even in the face of societal evils. Romans 8 gives us cause for celebration because, in spite of all that is going on in this world that is bad, the apostle Paul tells us of the eventual triumph of God.

For I reckon that the sufferings of this present time are not worthy to be compared with the glory which shall be revealed in us. For the earnest expectation of the creature waiteth for the manifestation of the sons of God.

For the creature was made subject to vanity, not willingly, but by reason of him who hath subjected the same in hope, Because the creature itself also shall be delivered from the bondage of corruption into the glorious liberty of the children of God. For we know that the whole creation groaneth and travaileth in pain together until now. And not only they, but ourselves also, which have the firstfruits of the Spirit, even we ourselves groan within ourselves, waiting for the adoption, to wit, the redemption of our body.

For we are saved by hope: but hope that is seen is not hope: for what a man seeth, why doth he yet hope for? But if we hope for that we see not, then do we with patience wait for it. . . .

> And we know that all things work together for good
> to them that love God, to them who are the called
> according to his purpose. (vv. 18–25, 28)

God is at work through His people. Christians are
crying out for justice and are changing the world. They
are evangelizing and building the church. But that does
not mean that we will bring in the Kingdom of God
without Jesus returning. Christians may be instru-
ments through which God builds His Kingdom, but not
until His Son returns to put down the evil kingdom
which is also growing will it be time for God's ultimate
party.

In the meantime, we must go to those in Ethiopia
who starve and feed them and tell them that a better
day is coming. We must go as servants to the oppressed
in the Gaza Strip and minister to them and explain to
them that a day of deliverance is at hand. We must go
to the lonely, the sick, and the dying, and tell them,
sometimes in words and sometimes by our deeds and
our presence, that they are loved. Insofar as it is possible, we must party with them. And as we do so, we
point beyond these limited signs of the Kingdom to the
great party that is on its way.

> Then cometh the end, when he [Jesus] shall have deliv-
> ered up the kingdom to God, even the Father; when he
> shall have put down all rule and all authority and
> power. For he must reign, till he hath put all enemies
> under his feet. (1 Cor. 15:24–25)

Chapter 11

ALL'S WELL
THAT ENDS WELL

Perhaps the most serious problem with talking about the Kingdom of God as a party is that the whole idea runs contrary to the work ethic that has been drilled into our consciousness. That work ethic has religious roots, as sociologists like Max Weber correctly discern. Particularly within the Calvinist tradition, people have endeavored to express their commitment to God through a commitment to work. Vocations of Christians have been looked upon as divinely ordained "callings," and Christian discipleship has been understood as the living out of those callings with zeal.

> And whatsoever ye do in word or deed, do all in the name of the Lord Jesus, giving thanks to God and the Father by him. (Col. 3:17)

The faithful Christian, according to Calvinistic thought, is one who is faithful on the job and who works with diligence, not only when the boss is watching but also when alone. The Christian worker knows that God is always watching and views labor as a gift that should be offered up to Him.

> Servants, be obedient to them that are your masters according to the flesh, with fear and trembling, in singleness of your heart, as unto Christ; Not with eyeservice, as menpleasers; but as the servants of Christ, doing the will of God from the heart; With good will doing service, as to the Lord, and not to men. (Eph. 6:5–7)

DEVELOPING A THEOLOGY OF PLAY

Actually, work is so much a part of what it means to be a Christian that many of us who are imbued with the faith find it difficult to stop working. If and when we do stop, we usually feel guilty. People do not know how to retire and, all too often, retirement leads to psychic death and even physical death. It is as though many of us cannot seem to find a reason for living once we lose our jobs. Work, for too many of us, is the only activity in which we feel we are glorifying God.

In light of the highly spiritual significance that Christians give to work, it is easy to see why they might have difficulty understanding the Kingdom of God as a party. After all, for too many people, the only alternative to work has been a form of playing marked by the kind of obscene consumerism that has lured many into destructive lifestyles.

The ads on television give seductive suggestions that, if bored, lonely people purchase the "right" things, they will experience the kind of partying that will feed their souls. They have seen the great American party which is built on escalating artificially created "wants" and which has led so many to waste their lives for things that do not satisfy (Isa. 55:2). They have seen so many of us lured into believing that only by getting a lot of money and buying all the things that the ads tell us that we have to have will we have the friends and the kinds of celebrations that will make life meaningful.

They themselves have tasted the materialistic consumption promoted by the media blitz that bombards us hourly, and have become concerned. If the kind of "fun times" viewed on TV are the only alternatives to work, it is easy to see why work-ethic Christians would condemn any suggestion that the Kingdom of God might be a party.

I recently received a letter that reflected that kind of reaction:

> God is working. Jesus is working. And the Holy Spirit is in us—working! I work. And when I am really depressed I work, really work . . . Please consider shelving your party message.

The perverted parties of this world had turned the writer off to all parties, and the only joy that she can find is in work.

For us to really get into the party which God has prepared for us, we need to develop a theology of play to go along with our theology of work. We must come to understand that play is much more than taking a deep breath between streaks of productive labor. We have to come to grips with the fact that play is a good thing in and of itself.

C. S. Lewis gives us some intimations of play in his book *Surprised by Joy*. He tells how play at its best can lift us out of time and space and place us in a rapturous state in which we taste something of the eternal. Peter Berger, in his book, *Rumors of Angels*, gives further explanation of this observation and goes so far as to claim that, when play is at its best, something of the presence of God breaks into our lives and redemptive powers are experienced. This is what God's kind of partying is supposed to do for us. At its best it is supposed to give us a taste of the glory that is to come. It ought to be a time when something of the celebration which is already going on in heaven breaks into our lives.

Allow me to share with you an experience from my college days. I was a basketball player on a not-too-good team that had losing seasons the entire four years I was in school. But in my senior year there was a game that for me was better than all the good games ever played put together. To quote from my college year-book:

> Best of all was the last game played against Eastern Baptist Seminary. With five minutes left all hope seemed gone as the Theologs held a thirteen-point advantage. But two minutes later, it was five points. Then Daryl Warren made two jump shots in rapid succession. Campolo's layup put us one thin point ahead. With seconds remaining, the Theologs reversed the lead with a field goal. We brought the ball in, Whitman shot and missed. The Theologs took the rebound and started down the floor. Then Campolo stole the ball and the victory with a frantic layup. All's well that ends well.

As the ball dropped through the hoop, it was party time. My teammates lifted me on their shoulders. My friends came flocking out of the stands. In the twinkling of an eye I was transported into ecstatic celebration. For me, that moment was lifted out of time; in it I tasted something of the glory that is to come when I will be caught up to be with Jesus and the saints in that blowout event to which theologians apply the dull label, "the eschaton."

There might be spiritual gratification in work, but in that playful victory celebration there was more than spiritual gratification. There was revelation. And if there is any consciousness of a lineal progression of time in heaven, I am sure that a billion years from now that eternalized moment of triumph that transpired years ago in a dingy college gym will still be with me. That partying moment is now part of who I am and what I am. In that moment, I was as alive as I could be this side of heaven, and in that moment there was a crack in time and space through which I glimpsed something of the party that is to come.

All of this is foreign to those of us who were raised on the Protestant work ethic and who are resistant to being acculturated into the consumer patterns that have been promoted in America since World War II. For us, work is what good people do. Even our concepts of heaven have been marked by this value orientation.

I can remember hearing sermons that were built around speculations as to what kind of work God would assign us in the afterlife. In one particular sermon, I recall that my pastor pointed out that God had great universes for us to administer and rule over in His name. For him, Heaven was a promotion to a top executive position which would make the corporate vice-presidencies that some of us did not get here on earth seem trivial by comparison. The heaven he preached was a workaholic's paradise. The idea that heaven might be primarily celebrating or partying with God would have been unthinkable to him. Yet that is what the Scriptures tell us about the life after life. It is a party!

And I heard as it were the voice of a great multitude, and as the voice of many waters, and as the voice of mighty thunderings, saying, Alleluia: for the Lord God omnipotent reigneth. Let us be glad and rejoice, and give honour to him: for the marriage of the Lamb is come, and his wife hath made herself ready. And to her was granted that she should be arrayed in fine linen, clean and white; for the fine linen is the righteousness of saints.

And he saith unto me, Write, Blessed are they which are called unto the marriage supper of the Lamb. And he saith unto me, These are the true sayings of God. (Rev. 19:6–9)

A Special Appendix

Throughout this book I have mentioned a mission organization I serve and to which I have given my life. It is the Evangelical Association for the Promotion of Education.

In Philadelphia and in Camden, New Jersey, we are working with scores of kids described by one judge in juvenile court as the "throw-away children." Many of them have been physically and sexually abused and all of them live out their lives in an environment of grinding poverty, drugs, and violence. We reach out to these kids with the story of Jesus, with love, and with a commitment to help. We have programs that include tutoring, athletics, camping, Bible study, cultural enrichment activities, and one-on-one counseling and evangelism. During the summer, when we are in high gear, we are working with as many as two thousand youngsters each day.

We also have a special Christian school for the kids who live in the government housing projects of the city. Right now we have kindergarten through fifth grade, but we will soon extend our school right through the high school grades.

Overseas in Haiti we have a network of schools that educate, feed, and evangelize more than three thousand children daily. Our three full-time workers in the field serve under the direction of Haitian pastors and coordinate all of this work in addition to supervising three clinics.

If you want to help in what we are doing, here are some things you might consider.

1. *Give and pray.* Ours in a relatively small organization so that every dollar given really counts. Small gifts can help bring God's party to small villages in Haiti and to deprived areas in urban America. Prayer is the primary thing that has kept us going through the years, so be sure to do it. If you want to pray for our specific needs and problems, write and get on our mailing list. We will send you our monthly newsletter.

2. *Volunteer.* We are always looking for people (primarily single) both young and old, who are willing to come work with us, both overseas and in urban America. We have a special need for those who are able to teach school in our own Cornerstone Christian Academy.

It is easy to correspond with us. Just write:

E.A.P.E.
Box 238
St. Davids, PA 19087